Partners and Ministers

Partners and Ministers

Ted Roberts

To Jack & Dai

*With deep gratitude
for your love &
fellowship in Christ.
A record of some
of the things we
have been through
together.*

*Ted
15 Sept. 72*

Falcon books · London

First published 1972
© Ted Roberts 1972

SBN 85491 824 8

Falcon Books are published by CPAS Publications, a department of the Church Pastoral Aid Society, Falcon Court, 32 Fleet Street, London EC4Y 1DB.

Overseas agents
EMU Book Agencies Ltd,
511 Kent Street, Sydney, NSW, Australia
CSSM and Crusader Bookroom Society Ltd,
177 Manchester Street, Christchurch, New Zealand
Sunday School Centre Wholesale,
PO Box 3020, Cape Town, South Africa

Printed in Great Britain by
Redwood Press Limited,
Trowbridge, Wiltshire

Contents

Foreword

It is a great joy to write about the experiment described in this book for, ever since I came to Stepney from Tanzania, I have had the privilege of being associated with it. I have come to know the men and their families as close personal friends.

I have been able, therefore, to test the validity of the whole scheme and of what is here claimed for it not from a distance (as bishop of the area in which it is taking place) but as a participant. Indeed, I think I can say that I am myself on trial in the pages of this book as much as the author and those he is writing about.

I am glad to be so closely involved in a plan for supplementary ministry in East London, for I believe in it with all my heart.

I am certain that if we are to act constructively to bridge the gulf between the Church and the working class we must above all else be ready to *experiment*. The shape of the Ministry in the institutional Church is already changing (together with much else which, a few years ago, appeared immutable) under social, economic and cultural pressures.

I believe that the Holy Spirit is compelling all of us who are involved in the mission of the Church to change our attitudes radically, because without such change there can be no hope of effective missionary work anywhere, least of all in East London.

In spite of the devotion of many great priests and ministers of the gospel who have spent their lives here, in spite of their readiness to share as fully as possible the hardships and the bitter poverty of the years before the Welfare State, in spite of large investment by the Church in buildings and staff, the Church since the Industrial Revolution has never been the Church of the working class. It is only if we recognize the extent and magnitude of this alienation that we can appreciate the urgency of the task.

Obviously a change in the pattern of ministry is not the only kind of change that is required. But it must have priority; for, without it, it is profoundly unlikely that the Christian community can change fast enough to be an effective instrument of the gospel. Time is *not* on our side. I pray that this book may be not only read, but used as a talking point, or even as an action point, wherever in our great cities its theme is relevant.

† Trevor Huddleston, C.R.,
Bishop of Stepney.

Introduction

Anyone who takes it upon himself to add to the mounting flood of books currently arguing reform of the church is, I believe, obliged to have good reason. It has always been easier to talk than to follow the Master. The temptations to bypass with words the demands of obedience are greater now than ever. The church is struggling for survival; should we not save our breath for the struggle?

My first ten years in East London have left me in no doubt that Christians are at this moment being faced with issues of life or death. In the midst of a huge city, it is impossible to avoid this conclusion. In the suburbs the traditional symbols of success may persist. But full churches and thriving organizations may obscure the danger, and its imminence. It is easy to assume that a shipwrecked sailor in a lifeboat is better off than his companion in the sea. But suppose the boat is leaking? Is he any better off then? At least the man in the water is learning to swim!

It seems that the signals regarding the desperate state of church life have reached the inner city sooner than suburbia. Perhaps Christians in the inner city are being forced by circumstances to adopt attitudes which seem strange to those who are still secure. But there is just the chance that in time some of our experience will be relevant to others.

The desire to share one lesson may be sufficient reason for yet another book. But why has it been written so soon? Is it right to do the sharing while the lesson is being learned? That question in turn raises many other questions.

The spiritual dangers of saying too much too soon have held us back for several years. At the same time, we have a responsibility which derives from the privilege of serving God in East London at this particular moment, and a debt which arises from having taken so long to learn so little.

If the struggle for survival is desperate, are there not many more important issues to be faced than the nature of the ministry? Probably yes, but we have discovered that in trying to solve this particular problem we have had to face many other questions about the church, all of which seem to us to be crucial.

Finally, there have been a whole group of questions arising from uncertainty about the scheme which have caused us to hang back from publicity.

Why should one little experiment in East London be of interest, when so many have done so much for so long to establish new and different forms of ministry?

Can we be sure that the men will eventually be ordained? If they are, will their partnership in the ministry achieve our objective, a stronger church?

I have tried to justify writing this book as an attempt to share some of the lessons learned. Even so, would it not have been wiser to wait?

Every Christmas my wife and I send our family and friends a photograph of our five children. It is usually taken in August, so it is out of date before it is sent. By the next Christmas the children will have changed unbelievably. Now and again, when visiting, they see themselves in a picture which is two or three years old. The experience never fails to raise a laugh. But, however much they may change, the basic facts remain the same. There are still five of them, three of one kind and two of the other.

Like a family, the church should, if it is alive, be growing and changing. The ministry in our two churches will have changed by the time you read this. I have added to the mounting flood of books and taken the risks involved in doing so at this particular time because, if the basic facts were true at the time of writing, they are still true now.

1 The Idea

Can a docker be a clergyman in the Church of England? Even if it were possible, is it desirable or necessary? Would it help to overcome the alienation of the working class from the church?

That is the sort of question I was asking myself when, in June 1969, I wrote to seven members of our two East London parishes inviting them to consider training for ordination.

Two clergymen and a parish worker had managed to do all that had been expected of them in the past, but for several years I had been wondering if men who were born and bred in the area should be brought into partnership in the ministry. Trevor Huddleston was our new bishop. I soon discovered that we shared a passion. The idea of an indigenous church, which was at the root of my thinking, had for years been a cherished principle of his work as a missionary in Africa. The church in rural Africa shares with the church in urban England one common factor, which we in England have been slow to accept: we are both missionary churches. Two societies, which at first sight could not be more different—Masasi and East London—in principle have the same need in common. If God is to be given His due glory, both communities must have a church which grows out of, and belongs in, the local community.

Overseas it has long been accepted that if a genuinely indigenous church is to grow it must have an indigenous ministry. After much painful change in thinking and attitudes, Western missionaries are accepting their servant role overseas. Africans must lead in Africa, Indians in India. We have failed to see that working class people are likewise best equipped to lead the church in the working class areas of Britain. We believe that the different societies in Nairobi and North-ampton demand different patterns of church life. Yet we go on expecting those patterns to be the same in the very different cultures of Bournemouth and Bow.

St Mark, Victoria Park is in Bow, St James the Less in Bethnal Green. Only two stations on the underground east of the heart of the City of London, we are proud inheritors of the true cockney tradition. If there are any Englishmen left with the 'coal in the bath, beware of footpads' image of 'the East End', they will be surprised when they visit us to find that the slums have nearly all been replaced by modern flats. The children are well dressed. People are enjoying their overdue affluence. This much is obvious even to a casual observer. It takes a little longer to find out that the taxi drivers, dockers, office cleaners and factory workers are not ashamed of being working class! In fact, if they have thought about it at all, they probably believe that their way of life is as valid and enjoyable as anyone else's. A Christian visiting East London will soon discover that, for the majority, the church does not constitute part of that way of life.

At first sight it seems unreasonable that the church should be so weak, bearing in mind the enormous efforts of earlier generations of Christians in the area. Since the beginning of the Industrial Revolution, much love and practical Christian concern has been lavished on East London. Vast sums of money have been spent by the church, and heroic work done by clergy and lay helpers, but little of this enormous effort has endured. Most East End parishes have records which bear great tribute to earlier generations of Christians. There will be memories of many miraculous conversions, of men called to the ministry, of missionaries serving overseas. Even in the darkest days of depression, God was glorified by the triumphs achieved in His name. But these achievements have been almost exclusively with individuals. For some reason we have failed to create Christian community. However sacrificial the service of those who have gone before, there seems to have been little to hand on to the next generation. The church simply has not taken root and thriven in East London.

It seemed to some of us that, if a way could be found to share the leadership of the church with people who really belonged to East London, perhaps we could take one step towards establishing a church that belongs.

This was the seed thought which led me to write to the seven men. Six accepted my invitation to begin training, two have since dropped out. One started a year behind the others, and the other three may well join the team when their circumstances change.

We like to think that this flexibility is typical of our attitude to the whole plan. When the time comes for ordination, each man will face a major personal commitment. Until then, we have tried to maintain as much freedom of decision as possible.

Jack is the oldest at 60 and is a docker. He left school at fourteen and served as a regular soldier in the Guards. In 1971 as a result of the run down of London docks he was made redundant, but he is no stranger to the dole queue, having been several times unemployed between the wars.

Bill is 40 and the single Grammar school boy. Born and bred in Bethnal Green, he is a telephone engineer with a special responsibility for training other Post Office staff in First Aid.

Henry is 35 and was born in India. His family settled in Stepney when India became independent. Henry was then 13 and his schooling was drastically interrupted. He married a school teacher, also a local girl, and earns his living servicing computers and business machines.

Gordon, aged 31, spends his working days on building sites, specializing in covering roofs with felt and bitumen. He was offered a Grammar school 'scholarship' but he is one of seven brothers, and the family budget would not allow him to take the opportunity.

All four are married with children; all, at least in some measure, work with their hands. Two have lived in the district all their lives. The two who were not actually born in East London have lived there most of their lives.

Training began in January 1970. It was understood from the outset that each man's call would have to be confirmed by the local church before he offered himself for selection by ACCM. The men accepted that by putting training before selection they risked working for a goal that they might not achieve. They believed that, even if there were no ordination at the end, the training would have been worthwhile.

In May 1971 every member of the two congregations was asked to express an opinion on the fitness of the men to serve as their ministers. This step required considerable preparation. The idea of local men as pastors was as new to them as it was to us. Questions about the scheme were collected, and answered later both in writing and at public meetings. The men explained their reasons for believing that they were called by God and offered to answer questions during an evening service.

During this time, while the scheme and the men were open to criticism, all concerned felt very sensitive. We decided it was good to be vulnerable in this way. We began to understand part of the New Testament as we had never done before. When Jesus began His public ministry, those among whom He had grown up said: 'Is not this Jesus, the son of Joseph, whose father and mother we know?' (John 6.42). It has now become obvious to us that the pain of that experience was a small price to pay for the confidence of knowing that you are accepted by those who know you best.

When the bishop counted the votes, he found that the church was in favour of each man going ahead for training with a view to his ordination for ministry in the local church. A week later the bishop explained to both congregations at a joint service that as members of the Anglican church they must accept that their decision was subject to the authority of the universal church. He represented the wider church, and he would be advised by a selection board appointed by the church's official body responsible for the ministry, the Advisory Council for the Church's Ministry (ACCM).

All four men went together to a selection conference in March 1972. Jack was recommended for training for the post-retirement ministry, the three others were approved for Auxiliary Pastoral Ministry.

The whole training programme is expected to last five years. After three of those five years the men will be made deacons. The final ordination to the priesthood should therefore take place at the end of 1974.

We soon realized that we should need a name. The choice of a proper title was difficult. Our objective was partnership, and if these men were to share the ministry with the existing staff there should be no difference, even in name. In practice it was obvious that, at least for the time being, they would need a distinctive title.

Auxiliary Pastoral Ministry is used to describe the officially established supporting ministry. But our plan is significantly different from APM. To use the same title would be confusing.

Begging a handful of questions, we could claim that our ministers will really be New Testament 'elders', but that name would also invite confusion. Its present use in nonconformist churches, the debate surrounding its use in the New Testament, and the simple fact of common English usage, rendered it useless for our purpose.

In the end, we settled for 'Supplementary' ministry. This is the title used in the report *A Supporting Ministry* (ACCM, 1968). This report of the Welsby Committee was decisive in our early days of planning. We don't like the name very much; it is not beautiful and, as Owl said to Pooh, 'it takes a good deal of pencil to say a long thing like that'. But until we can find a better name, or do without the distinction, it will have to do.

Our plan has been described simply, without explanation or justification, because the reader needs this information if he is to make sense of the arguments which follow. Now it is necessary to explain our reasons for wanting to create this kind of team ministry, and what we hope to achieve by it.

2 The Novelty of the Scheme

During the past few years we have discovered a growing interest in Supplementary Ministry. We have all enjoyed answering questions about our scheme, and have learned many useful lessons from these conversations. One fact which has emerged very clearly is that most Christians have a fixed and very limited idea of the ministry. Good books have been written on patterns of ministry, several important reports have been produced, pioneering work has been done by worker priests, industrial missions and the Southwark Ordination Course, but the fact remains that the vast majority of those asked, 'What is an Anglican clergyman?' would reply by describing a stereotype.

He has been trained in a college. He is a professional in the sense that Christian ministry is the full time work for which he is paid. He would normally expect to stay in one parish for five to ten years and then move on. If he is not already in sole charge of a parish, he would expect to be eventually, therefore he must be equipped to do all the things that are part of a minister's normal work.

This type of minister has served the church well. To propose an alternative is not to suggest that we can do without him. On the contrary, it seems likely that an effective Supplementary Ministry will demand full time clergy more skilled and gifted than ever. But we have no right at all to suppose that the present pattern of full time ministry should be the only ministry.

Many clergymen complain that they find themselves doing everything but the job they were trained and ordained to do. It has been our experience that, both in training the team and in being its resource man, the full time minister is spiritually and intellectually stretched. In meeting the needs of the part time team he finds himself doing those things he is best qualified to do.

In arguing the value of a team of part time ministers we are not arguing against the full time clergyman. It is not a case of 'either or' but 'both together'. The Biblical picture is of 'varieties of ministry'. Our inherited notion is crippling because it is rigid, settled and inflexible. The New Testament pattern, by contrast, is one of variety, fluidity, openness to change. We have imposed upon ourselves an invariable pattern of hierarchy. The alternative is excitingly liberating.

In the New Testament for example, a man is called to use his particular gift. There is both itinerant ministry and settled ministry. Some are paid by the church, some are not. One thing is certain, that those who visited temporarily from outside were not regarded as 'the Ministry'. The local church normally produced its own ministry from within. But however varied the Biblical patterns, our accepted idea of the ministry is fixed and limited.

Our plan for Supplementary Ministry suggests one alternative; there are many others. Our arguments for this particular form of part time ministry will be made by contrasting this pattern with the existing full time ministry. It is a convenient way of presenting the case. Our present pattern is a useful point of reference, something we all have in common. In making the contrast, we are not wanting to argue that one is better than the other; certainly not that one is exclusive of the other. A balanced ministry will be varied, it must have many different forms.

Our scheme is different from the traditional pattern of ministry in six ways:

1 A team rather than solitary ministers

We have become so familiar with the idea of one man in sole charge of one parish that the idea of inviting four men to share that ministry may well seem extravagant. I was appointed, according to tradition, to be vicar of the two parishes in plurality, and have shared that ministry over the years with a succession of able curates and church workers. From time to time one of the curates would be appointed curate-in-charge of St Mark's, but there was never any doubt that I was the person ultimately responsible, under the bishop, for the cure of souls in both places. In the next chapter three reasons will be given for radically changing this pattern.

2 Call by the local church rather than outside appointment

On that Sunday in May 1971 when the men stood before the people who knew them so well and asked for a decision for or against their ordination, we all felt a totally unexpected sense of excitement. We certainly had no intention of making history, we were just doing what seemed right, even necessary. We had not seriously searched for one, but we knew of no precedent. In the past, ministers had been sent to the parish. The church members had not known where they had come from. They accepted in faith that they had been called by God. Now they suddenly found that this call to the ministry and to the parish was something about which every member of the church was expected to have an opinion.

3 Settled rather than itinerant ministry

You will remember that the traditional minister expects to move around from place to place during his ministry. Bishops have tended to discourage a man from serving in his own parish after his ordination. Given the pattern of professional ministry, there are good arguments to support this policy. There is also a strong case to be made for men who have been born and bred in the area sharing the ministry with the man from 'outside'. Our Supplementary Ministers believe they are called to the local church. They have no desire to offer themselves as ministers to any other congregation. What will happen if they change jobs or move will be dealt with in Chapter 4.

4 Training—local and practical

There are two ways in which our plan differs from the traditional pattern in regard to training. The present full time minister expects to go away to college for two, three or maybe five years. Our men hope to learn all that they will need to know while living a normal family life and doing a daily job, in the local situation where they expect to exercise their ministry.

While he is away at college, the traditional professional minister is expected to complete a course which is largely academic. Most will be expected to pass examinations. If, in order to minister in the local church, our men had to submit to an exam oriented study course, they would have little hope of success. While we expect our ministers to be able to take sole charge of any parish in the land, some minimum standard must be demanded, and it is hard to see how the present system could be fundamentally altered. Once accept that there is a place for the local minister supplementing the work of the full time man, and a different type of training is not only possible but desirable.

5 A specific term of service rather than open ended commitment

It is generally accepted that ordination commits a man to the ministry for life. While exceptions do obviously occur, permanence is the norm. The Supplementary Ministers have willingly accepted a limitation of seven years upon their licence to officiate, after which it will be reviewed and may or may not be renewed.

We are therefore suggesting that we follow a pattern which is the opposite of the tradition. Rather than permanence as the norm with short term service the exception, we argue for short time service as the norm and accept the possibility that a man may serve all his life.

We have tried to separate this issue from the vexed question of the indelibility of orders, which is discussed in Chapter 4.

6 Voluntary rather than paid

The fact that Supplementary Ministers will not receive any salary is certainly not a distinctive feature of our scheme. This principle has been well established by many men over the years. But it is a particularly important issue in East London. It is therefore listed among the characteristics of our scheme which differ from the pattern, in order that the subject may be discussed more fully in the next chapter.

3 The Reasons for its Novelty

There are those who think that 'challenging the structures' is the latest fad, a party game for the younger generation. Understandably, the eagerness with which some attack well tried institutions provokes others to their defence. Action and reaction are equal and opposite. It is almost inevitable that opponents take up established positions and simply refuse to listen to each other, but then the real issues become obscured, and a valuable case may well go by default. A heavy responsibility rests upon those who propose change to prove their case; those who oppose it are likewise obliged to give proper reasons for their opposition.

In the previous chapter six ways were listed in which Supplementary Ministry differs from the traditional pattern of full time ministry. In this chapter it is hoped to justify these differences. But first a preliminary point must be established.

1 The alienation of the working class

It is apparent that for a very large proportion of the population of England the organized church is particularly irrelevant because of the issue of class. To speak of class never fails to cause confusion. It nearly always generates heat. Many of us would like to remove the word from our vocabulary, but before we can do that we must remove the experience from our lives. In a group of which I am a member comparison was drawn between the dividing line in South African society, which is colour, and in London where it is class. Someone who had lived in South Africa said that there at least the church is established on both sides of the division. In London the church cannot claim even tentatively, to be so bilaterally based. Another member observed,

'The difference in South Africa is not greater. It is more obvious. Our problems are more complex and are likely to be more enduring'.

Paul singled out the three great divisions in society—race, class and sex—when he said, 'There is neither Jew nor Greek, there is neither slave nor free, there is neither male nor female; for you are all one in Christ Jesus' (Galatians 3.28).

Some Christians would suggest that this means we should not talk about class because, once we are in Christ, the division no longer exists. Unfortunately this is not so. This Scripture is saying that these divisions are all too real, they have always been part of the fabric of society; but a Christian should not allow them to affect his relationships with those who are different because of race, class or sex. Divisions of class do not go away just because we pretend they are not there, any more than the divisions of race or sex. The church in East London is weak because we have managed to ignore differences of class. By ignoring them we have allowed them to affect our attitudes and encouraged the church to reflect patterns of life which are foreign to East London.

Bishop E. R. Wickham writes, 'The working class, whatever its transmutations, has remained the largest single social group most estranged from the churches of Europe'.[1] The one notable exception has been the Roman Catholic Church. It is worth noticing that the Roman Catholic Church in Ireland was not identified with the English ruling classes. Therefore when large groups of Irish immigrants found themselves concentrated in the worst housing areas of London, Glasgow and Liverpool, their priests were not identified with the employers. First they came from Ireland, then later from within their own urban communities. Their priesthood was indigenous.

Charles Booth records the historical roots of our present problems in East London. He found that churches, missions and settlements could gather a respectable congregation of the poor by liberal granting of relief. The missions and settlements with their large staffs from outside the area only helped to mask the real problem, the absence of responsible adult church life. Booth says, 'Wherever the regular working class is found . . . it seems equally impervious to the claims of religion . . . while those who do join any church become almost indistinguishable from the class with which they then mix, The change that has really come about is not so much *of* as *out of* the class to which they have belonged'.[2]

There are exceptions to this pattern of working class alienation. The Durham miners, the chapels of the Welsh valleys or Lancashire mill towns are often quoted, but these examples relate to small industrial towns. A city of half a million does not always break up into one class areas, a vast metropolis like London does. This is our problem in East London. Willmott and Young[3] describe East London as a vast one class quarter. It is wrong to impose on these areas patterns of church life which reflect values more middle class than biblical, and expect them to take root. This is what we have done when we have unthinkingly transplanted churches which fit a middle class way of life and therefore appeal to middle class people. What we should do is to encourage the growth of indigenous churches in working class areas. We must apply at home the lessons we have learned on the overseas mission field. A strong church will become established and will expand according to the laws of spiritual life when it is allowed to reflect those aspects of its community's own culture which are consistent with biblical principles.

The complex and emotive theme of class has probably never been described better than by Richard Hoggart in *The Uses of Literacy*.[4] He argued that the 'educators', among whom the clergy are a significant group, will always be tempted to see this distinct working class culture as 'inferior'—particularly if they have themselves been educated 'out of it'. In the *Observer* Hoggart wrote, 'Grammar schools can exert a great—if well meant or even unconscious—pressure to remove their working class pupils from attachment to their homes and neighbourhoods; they tend to seek to attach them to middle class values . . . a substantial proportion (of the teachers) not only reject their own working class background, but reject it with scorn and adhere grimly to their new middle class attitudes'.[5]

A similar process has been at work in the church. It has been enforced by the fact that many of the clergy are themselves educated in the atmosphere described by Hoggart. Whatever may or may not happen in the schools, the church is committed to the view that 'there is neither Jew nor Greek, there is neither slave nor free'. One culture is

no better than the other. Both working class and middle class have
their strengths and weaknesses, neither is wholly good or wholly bad.
But they are different. J. H. Goldthorpe and D. Lockwood summarize
evidence on the effect of a person's own perception of the class structure
from research in England, Germany and Switzerland.[6]

Although conducted entirely independently of each other, the
findings in all three countries are essentially comparable, both in their
approach and their findings. They are probably the clearest indications
available of the basic differences in the social perspectives of working
and middle class people.

It was discovered that the majority of people have a more or less
clearly defined image of society as being stratified in some way or
other; that is to say, they are aware of inequalities in the distribution
of wealth, prestige and power. Some see this division in terms of two
contending sections differentiated by the possession or non-possession
of power. Others have an image of society as an extended hierarchy
primarily identified in terms of prestige. Generally speaking, working
class people are more likely to hold the power image, middle class
people that of prestige.

On the basis of this research it is possible to illustrate one aspect of
class consciousness in the following way:[7]

WORKING CLASS VIEW	MIDDLE CLASS VIEW
GENERAL BELIEFS	
The social order is divided into 'us' and 'them'; those who do not have authority and those who do. The division between 'us' and 'them' is virtually fixed, at least from the point of view of one man's life chances. What happens to you depends a lot on luck; otherwise you have to learn to put up with things.	The social order is a hierarchy of differentially rewarded positions; a ladder containing many rungs. It is possible for individuals to move from one level of the hierarchy to another. Those who have ability and initiative can overcome obstacles and create their own opportunities. Where a man ends up depends on what he makes of himself.

WORKING CLASS VIEW	MIDDLE CLASS VIEW

GENERAL VALUES

'We' ought to stick together and get what we can as a group. You may as well enjoy yourself while you can instead of trying to make yourself 'a cut above the rest'.

Every man ought to make the most of his own capabilities and be responsible for his own welfare. You cannot expect to get anywhere in the world if you squander your time and money. 'Getting on' means making sacrifices.

ATTITUDES ON MORE SPECIFIC ISSUES

on the best job for a son

'A trade in his hands'. 'A good steady job'.

'As good a start as you can give him'. 'A job that leads somewhere'.

towards people needing social assistance

'They have been unlucky'. 'They never had a chance'. 'It could happen to any of us'.

'Many of them had the same opportunities as others who have managed well enough'. 'They are a burden on those who are trying to help themselves'.

on Trade Unions

'Trade Unions are the only means workers have of protecting themselves and of improving their standard of living'.

'Trade Unions have too much power in the country'. 'The Unions put the interests of a section before the interests of the nation as a whole'.

Clearly these are two sharply contrasting social perspectives, each of which comprises a set of internally consistent beliefs, values and attitudes.

Confusion arises because there are so many different ways of identifying class. Confusion becomes confounded when the problems

of definition become overlaid with our own passionate, often un-
confessed, prejudices. Education is a useful vehicle for illustrating the
problem because, while the schools face difficulties similar to the
churches, clergymen can be a little more objective about the teachers'
problems than they can about their own.

In his article, *The Dead End Kids*,[8] Albert Rowe, headmaster of the
David Lister School, Hull, is concerned about those pupils, mostly
from working class homes, who become most difficult to deal with in
their last year because they are bored, indifferent or actively hostile.
The key is building the right relationship with these pupils. This is
based on accepting them without reservation on the two grounds on
which they are commonly rejected—cultural and academic. It is in
these two areas that the church has most commonly rejected working
class Christians.

'Cultural first. Their working class culture should be accepted to be
as valid as anyone else's, which it in fact is. Not inferior, simply
different. The theory that they are culturally-deprived, which they
are in certain respects, has unfortunately been taken also to mean
that their feelings, experience, responses and outlook are inferior—
that they are inferior as human beings.

'Wearing the blinkers of the middle class, teachers have traditionally
misunderstood their culture, condemned it, and tried to change it to
their own supposedly superior one. But the pupils can't change it.
Nor would they even if they could—it would be an utter betrayal of
all they hold dear. They therefore, in turn, reject the teachers' middle
class culture. So the barrier is set up which makes all communications
and all real learning impossible.

'The teacher's task is to acknowledge the validity of working class
culture and to build upon the feelings, experiences, responses, and
views of themselves, life, and society the pupils have. Their culture
doesn't need changing in its fundamentals; the aim should be to
sensitize it and substantially expand and enrich it. In this as in other
matters we've got to get rid of our determination to allocate rank—this
group's culture is highest, that group's next, and so on down the scale.'

Mr Rowe goes on to argue that working class ways of speech, for
example, are just as valid as any other, because they enable people to

communicate effectively. The clothes, magazines and records they buy are genuinely believed by the pupils to be the best. To reject their values out-of-hand is tantamount to rejecting them. The church, no less than the school, has rejected people because it rejects their tastes. The pupils want respect, so do working class Christians. How can people, in school or church, act responsibly if they are not respected and treated responsibly? By assuming that some tastes are superior we automatically convey the notion that the one whose tastes are inferior is an inferior person.

Mr Rowe continues: 'Our education system is still tightly geared to the old static, closed, and privileged form of society, and not to the new dynamic and open form in which privilege has to be won and justified. This is seen most clearly in the examination system, which at present identifies as failures 50 per cent of pupils without even giving them the chance of taking part, thus rejecting them and convincing them that they're educational as well as examination failures, a very different thing.'

When the church allows itself to be geared to 'a static, closed and privileged form of society', it is also guilty of rejecting people. This rejection is felt, for example, if we say that a man must achieve a certain academic standard before he can be ordained.

What Mr Rowe says about the working class adolescent alienated from school could equally be said of the working class adult alienated from the church. The clergyman, like the teacher, must lose his class prejudice and learn to accept those who, on middle class values, are rejected.

2 Six particular advantages

The alienation of the working class from the church demands an indigenous church in those areas where we have imposed patterns of church life which are culturally foreign. Since an indigenous church must have an indigenous ministry, this need is a fundamental argument for Supplementary Ministry. The six potential advantages listed in the previous chapter will now be justified in detail.

(i) *a team*

The inherited pattern of ministry is for one man to be in sole charge of one parish. We believe that there are strong arguments for creating teams of part time and full time ministers.

(a) because of past experience

The pressures and demands of the ministry make the fellowship of a team essential. The sharing of insights and mutual support of intimate partners has been proved by experience to be vital. Those who share the burden must share the pain; the whole team therefore must share the responsibility if they are to support each other effectively. It is only as one experiences personally the joy and sorrow of the work of ministry that it becomes possible to share it with another. I believe that many a clergyman presses diocesan authorities for money to pay staff, not because the parish needs another full time minister, but because he needs a partner. I know several men who have tried valiantly to go it alone, only to become victims of physical, mental or spiritual attacks which they might have avoided if they had been able to share the burden effectively.

During our period of training, our group has built up such a depth of understanding that we are now capable of sharing the most intimate experiences and insights. Even if some other duties have had to lose priority in the process, the work done together in the group has been valuable for its own sake. And the work the men do will more than make up for what I have been unable to do during the training period. It has been a sound investment of my time to concentrate on the building of the team.

(b) because God's gifts are varied

Any clergyman would admit that he does not personally possess all the spiritual gifts necessary for the exercise of an effective ministry. But that is what we assume when we make one man alone responsible for the ministry in a parish.

The catalogue of the Spirit's gifts in Ephesians 4 suggests that a balanced ministry must be a corporate affair: 'His gifts were that some should be apostles, some prophets, some evangelists, some pastors and teachers' (Ephesians 4.11).

The creation of a team of ministers assumes that each recognizes that he may only have one gift, but that added to the others his gift helps to create a complete ministry. At a stroke we relieve one man of the tension of being unable to achieve the impossible, and liberate the individual gifts of many who would individually be ignored.

We have often been asked, 'What will they do?' They will certainly be much more than auxiliaries to the full time ministry. The team is a partnership, not a hierarchy. If they were allowed to lapse into a group of assistants to help out on Sundays, we would have failed twice over: once by falling from a higher ideal, and again by confirming many of the false assumptions about the church which we have deliberately set out to challenge.

A positive idea of what they will do demands a clear picture of what the church should be doing in an urban working class community. There is an enormous range of needs, each of which offers an opportunity for initiative. Each initiative demands initiators. One list which has already been suggested includes:

CHRISTIANS AT WORK

Understanding where power lies
Money
Relationships, e.g.
　Management/shop-floor
Task of Shop Stewards
Responsible work

CHRISTIANS AT WORSHIP

Prayer
Understanding and partici-
　pating in liturgy
House churches
Music
Experimental worship

CHRISTIANS IN DISCIPLESHIP
SITUATIONS

Bible studies
Discussion groups
Topic courses

CHRISTIANS AND NEIGHBOURHOOD
INSTITUTIONS

Borough Council
Tenants' Associations
Community development
Schools
Secular youth clubs

CHRISTIANS AND MINORITY
  GROUPS
  Immigrants
  Squatters
  Unemployed

CHRISTIANS AND CHURCH
  ORGANIZATIONS
  Children
  Young people
  Old people

CHRISTIANS AND MAINTENANCE
  Church buildings

CHRISTIANS AND HEALING WORK
  Alcoholics
  Drug addicts
  Discharged prisoners
  Unmarried mothers

CHRISTIANS KNOWING
  THEMSELVES
  Small group work
  Pastoral care and counselling

CHRISTIANS AND THE WIDER
  CHURCH
  The church overseas
  Other denominations
    locally

CHRISTIANS PROCLAIMING
  THEIR FAITH
  Evangelistic projects
  'Open' home meetings

CHRISTIANS AND THE ISSUES IN
  THE COMMUNITY
  Housing
  Education

If we take seriously the need to have a ministry which can provide knowledge and effective leadership in such a range of interests, it will be obvious that one person cannot cope. Probably the total (ordained and lay) ministry of one parish cannot cope. Certainly there will be no shortage of 'parcels of work' for gifted Christians to do. Most important, to this list must be added the involvement in spontaneous happenings in the street, the dropping in on neighbours and being dropped in on.

(ii) Call by the local church
It soon became obvious that Supplementary Ministry would not work without the enthusiastic support of the two churches. Unless

the congregations were prepared to accept these men, they would have
no ministry. As we worked our way through the problems of how to
canvass the opinion of the local churches and enlist their support, we
realized that we were rediscovering an ancient and important principle.
It was as though we had uncovered a fossil which suddenly came alive.
New Testament Christians expected to share in the appointment of
their ministers; somewhere we had allowed the principle to die. The
principle came alive when the men realized their need to know that
their ministry was accepted among their own people. For the people
to discover at the same time that they have an effective say in the
ordering of their own affairs was a revelation. Working class Christians
were being taken seriously at last.

The lists of qualifications for ministry in 1 Timothy 3 and Titus 1
have often been used as an ideal to set before a young man as he
begins his ministry. We tell him that he should aim to be 'not arrogant
or quick tempered or a drunkard or violent or greedy for gain, but
hospitable, a lover of goodness, master of himself . . .' (Titus 1.7–8).

Now suppose we see these words not directed to a young man as a
standard at which he must aim, but written to guide the local church in
the sort of men they should choose to be their ministers? We found that
we were able to read these words in that way. It was a joyful experience, a discovery which increased our confidence that we were doing
the right thing. The men standing in front of us were just such men.
There was no need to hope that they would turn out according to the
Bible's pattern; we knew them intimately and knew how far in practice or potential they measured up to that standard.

The principle that the local church should share in the call of men
to the ministry has not been entirely lost from the Church of England.
It is preserved in the shape of si quis—a good name for a fossil! In
fact, this legal vestige is more like the human appendix, a normally
useless organ which is liable to cause considerable inconvenience if it
ever goes wrong. A man about to be ordained is required to have read
in his local church an announcement of that fact inviting 'whosoever'
(Latin si quis) knows any impediment to his ordination to signify that
fact to the bishop. The congregation there do not have to be consulted.
They are not expected to have a view about the fitness of the man who

is to be their minister. Indeed, they are unlikely to meet him until after he has been ordained.

Uncontrolled congregationalism, when the congregation lacks spiritual life, can inhibit the freedom of a minister of vision and spiritual power. The balance of congregational and episcopal authority which is, in theory, at the heart of Anglicanism should guard against the weakness inherent in either alone. In the matter of the appointment of ministers, nothing but good can come from restoring to the local church its share of authority.

(iii) Local roots

(a) local insight is essential

A team of men born and bred in the area bring to the ministry valuable gifts of insight and experience. According to our inherited pattern a minister comes from 'outside'. He brings to a local church certain gifts and skills given by God and developed during his training at college. Supplementary Ministry does not question the continuing need for such men. In fact a team of local ministers will provide a full time minister with much greater opportunities to exercise those gifts and skills. But by combining 'local' and 'outside' ministry in one team, each enriches the other.

The church is beginning to grasp the value of leadership based on the principle 'let be'. In certain circumstances a leader's task is to create conditions in which other people's gifts can develop. The 'enabler' gives confidence, support and training to others. For too long we have behaved as though only one man has any gifts in any one congregation, however loudly we may have protested otherwise.

Most of my time in East London has been spent discovering my shortcomings. I have had to learn that the church needs the special insights which can only come from those born and bred in the district. I have had to face the fact that many of my middle class attitudes—nourished by my college training—were a positive disadvantage once I accepted the fact that my task was to encourage the growth of an indigenous church.

For example, over a period of years the life of the church at St Mark's declined to the point where I was prepared to argue that it should be closed. When all but nominal supervision from the clergy was withdrawn, the seeds sown by staff members over the years began to grow. Local leadership emerged, initiative was provoked and an indigenous church of forty adults, nearly all recent converts, has slowly been established.

When arguing for Supplementary Ministry I am certainly not denying the value of the itinerant professional clergyman; rather contending that his value will be increased once he learns to exercise his ministry within a local team.

(b) local strength emerges

An interesting example of the value of a local ministry emerged during the course of our training programme. One of the men was responsible for a service of naming and blessing for a child. Two days after he had taken the service, the baby died. The agony he felt and his sense of his own weakness was increased by the fact that they were his neighbours, only a few doors down the street. Whereas I could have retired behind the doors of the vicarage after expressing my regret at the tragedy, he did not have the protection of 'professionalism' and had to share his weakness with the rest of the church. It may well be that in this way 'weakness' became 'strength'. Sometimes the sheer pressure of facing another human being at moments of tragedy or joy forces a clergyman to grow a veneer of assumed 'strength' which can easily become insensitivity. It may even appear to those on the receiving end to be insincerity. A team of local ministers are not automatically immune from this disease, but they do stand a better chance of resisting it. They know they are weak; they are not being forced by others to appear to be strong; and having learned to share experiences during training they know that in the group there is the acceptance which will allow them to confess their weakness and discover the strength of Christ. 'I will all the more gladly boast of my weaknesses, that the power of Christ may rest upon me . . . for when I am weak, then I am strong' (2 Corinthians 12.9–10).

(c) the 'clergy line' is challenged

A local ministry will also help to break down the false division between clergy and laity. This problem is certainly not peculiar to working class areas. Most Christians share the horror of the 'clergy line' which separates clergy from laity. But the problem is more acute in working class areas because we have to add another element to all the other factors which create this 'line'. One clergyman in Liverpool claimed that what made him different from his neighbours was not the fact that he was a Christian, but that he was the only man in his parish who did not work with his hands.

The church is charged to confront the world with the offence of Christ; we obscure the 'stumbling block' of the cross when we give the impression that a follower of Christ is different from others in a way which has nothing to do with being a Christian. Many laymen want to keep the clergy special, dignified and different. Local ministers will have to face particular difficulties in this respect. They are not a class apart, but there will be those who will expect them to behave as though they are.

What will be the effect on working class men of their being designated leaders in the church, even though they are not being withdrawn to a residential college for training? There is evidence that when men are designated as Trade Union leaders they change their life style and to an extent no longer see things the same way as their members— though some firmly try to resist this. A man's frame of reference will be changed if he spends a lot of time, for example, at Party Conferences or Church Synods. When he is a designated leader, he takes on a new role. He is not reacting to decisions; he is making them. This adds up to what the French worker priests fear, who have argued against ordinary working class men being ordained. They fear that it will bring them over to 'the other side'.

But can Christian leadership be rooted in working class life without such ordination being part of the programme? Bishop E. R. Wickham, who formerly opposed a French-style priest-worker movement in this country, is ready to see the matter debated again. He notes the fact that though the number of clergy in secular jobs increases, few become engineers and factory workers. They are more likely to teach liberal studies in technical colleges! 'From the evidence it would seem that if the Church of England wanted genuine priest-*workers*, as a presence among industrial workers, she would have to find laymen there already and ordain them—though whether the good laymen ... should be allowed to lose their genuine lay status, and cease therefore to be models of what laymen can be, is highly questionable'. Later he returns to the subject, depressed by English failures to grasp the opportunities in the industrial world. 'It is for such depressing reasons that, *faute de mieux*, we must look again at models of more radical mission, and therefore at the idea of a more indigenous ministry, "in strength", such as the term "priests in secular employment" might mean'.[9]

(d) Congregational authority is encouraged.
The Church of England is both local and catholic, congregational and episcopal. To hold both truths in balance has never been easy. A ministry sent to the local church from 'outside' with episcopal authority as its only warrant, is evidence that at this point the scales are weighed heavily in favour of the catholic emphasis. A locally recruited ministry would add much needed weight to the congregational side of the balance.

(e) Local initiative is released
Probably the strongest argument for the creation of a local ministry in partnership with the existing 'mobile resource man' is to be found in the enormous fund of talent and energy waiting to be used. It has already been argued that men with individual gifts will be encouraged to take their share of leadership when they discover that they do not have to be 'all rounders'. A team gives a man security to offer a contribution he would be shy of making alone. There is also a whole field of leadership potential to be explored once we begin to look more closely at the sort of leader required in an indigenous working class church.

Some sociologists make a distinction between two groups of urban working class people and call them, with their customary charm, status assenting and status dissenting.

Status assenters will be proud of being working class, conscious of their tradition and anxious to preserve it. They reject middle class values and cherish the privilege of being one of 'us' rather than one of 'them'.

Status dissenters will be 'on the move' through the class structure, anxious to 'better themselves'. Their interests will be home centred and they will be very conscious of standards of morals, appearances, and family life. They will be more concerned about their children's education than their neighbours are. They are wanting something different, and will certainly ensure that, even if they do not succeed in crossing the boundary from working to middle class during their life time, their children will succeed in doing so.

The church has always appealed more to status dissenters than assenters. Indeed, because it is predominantly a middle class institution, the church can be used, often unconsciously, by those who are 'on the move', as a rung on the ladder of progress. The result of this appeal to one group has been to reinforce the attitude of the other group who reject the church as alien to their values. The creation of a team of local ministers will be understood by the status assenters as a gesture of confidence in them. They have not, on the whole, been encouraged to take a lead in the church before. This will be a step towards creating a church more working class than middle class, which will in turn attract those who assent to their own traditions.

No one would suggest that the ordination of a handful of local men is likely to oust overnight generations of rooted prejudice; but it is at least a step in that direction.

(iv) The training needs

Supplementary Ministry has given us an opportunity to experiment with training methods different from those used for training full time ministers. At one time we wondered whether any formal training was required at all. By laying stress on the training *we* give, we could stifle the natural gifts and aptitudes which are the essence of a local ministry. The apostles' training programme was three years in the company of the greatest teacher the world has known; but their training was informal, they learned by interpreting everyday events in the light of Scripture.

With some misgivings we settled for a five year training programme.

We have tried to follow Biblical precedent, however. Firstly, we have always tried to bear in mind that life and experience, interpreted by the Holy Spirit, are to be preferred to any syllabus of study we may be able to produce. Secondly, we have tried, however feebly, to copy Christ's pattern and to think of ourselves as a group of friends gathered round Himself, 'learning by experience'. Time alone will tell how far we achieved these high ideals. We have certainly made many mistakes. It is because we do not want costly mistakes to be wasted that we explain our programme here in some detail. This is done under two headings to demonstrate the two ways in which what we have tried to do differs most from traditional training.

(a) at home rather than at college

To send our four men away to residential college, even if they could have qualified for entrance, would have uprooted them from their environment and robbed them of their greatest single qualification for ministry: their identification with the local community. The experience of Abbé Michonneau must be quoted verbatim: 'Everything about our training seems pointed to a final product which will be polished to a bright middle class lustre. In the face of this we express surprise when our "graduates" are unwilling to go back to their native working class. We have made this practically impossible.'[10]

The removal of the men to college would also have robbed four wives of their husbands, twelve children of their fathers. Going away would have created complex difficulties for men who accept that one of the fundamental tests of a man's suitability for ministry is the way he orders his own home. 'He must manage his own household well, keeping his children submissive and respectful in every way; for if a man does not know how to manage his own household, how can he care for God's church?' (1 Timothy 3.4–5).

Granting the argument that training must be based on experience, it follows that the training must happen where the experience is to be found, in the local church. Since their goal is solely ministry in the local church, it also follows that effective training is best done in the place where the work will be done.

So far we have had to make no call on the national church for finance, and we hope to complete the training without having done so. In fact, expenses have been so slight that they have been met mainly by the men themselves with a little help from parish funds. At a time when costs of college training are constantly rising, this saving of money, while not essential to our argument, cannot be ignored.

The training differs from custom, not only in its location but also in its method.

(b) practical rather than academic

Conventional training for the ministry assumes an ability to pass examinations. By definition, East London is an area from which those who 'get on' educationally move out. One of the facts which has bedevilled the life of the church in the inner city is the tendency of the status dissenters, to whom the church at present most naturally appeals, to do well at school, 'better themselves', and move out to the suburbs. This is all part of the continuing process of weakening the church in the vast one class communities described earlier. This is not to say that some of our men could not, with effort, pass exams. They could and would if that were necessary. But it is not necessary. In fact, to submit themselves to the traditional patterns of academic training would be to alienate them from the very people they are called to serve.

To insist on practical rather than academic training is not to opt for a second best. On the contrary, we believe that the health of the church in working class areas demands that we recognize that there is indigenous leadership with intelligence and ability which cannot be measured by academic yardsticks. The call to be 'kings and priests' to be responsible in the world and in the church, is a call to all Christians, not just those who have five 'O' levels and two 'A' levels.

Another advantage of practical training becomes obvious once the distinction between expressive and instrumental leadership is accepted. An instrumental leader is someone who can organize and get things done. In the church he will need to be an 'all rounder', and therefore to have had some academic training. An expressive leader is the sort of person who can inspire others and lead thinking. While the instrumental leader may be chairman of the tenants' association, the expressive leader is more likely to be able to interpret what happened at the meeting, afterwards in the pub. The local church needs both kinds of leadership, but we have tended to exclude the expressive leader by an overemphasis on education. By creating a team of leaders, we are able to contain the expressive leader and enable him to function in a way that he could not do alone. When we insist on a single minister in charge of a parish by himself, we demand an instrumental leader who must have had a certain type of education. The creation of a team and a practical training programme together make it possible for the church to use a rich source of potential leadership, so far largely neglected.

At the beginning of our training, we worked out together a job specification. In this we tried to define precisely what a minister should do and what skill and knowledge he would need. We accepted that we would not all be expected to do all the duties listed, but only those for which our gifts equipped us. By subtracting each man's present capability from the lists of gifts and skills required to perform the duties expected of him, we arrived at his personal training need. This varies with each individual.

For example, Jack is more obviously a pastor than a preacher. He needs to be trained to apply the Scripture to people's individual needs; there is no need to burden him with the theory of homiletics. There are others, better able to preach, who would not be as effective as he is with people face to face. Bill's natural gifts lie in the direction of organization, and he should be encouraged to develop administrative skills; again, there is no need to burden others with this training when the tasks are ones for which they have little natural aptitude.

By referring to a man's training need from time to time, we hope to be able to ensure that we concentrate the time available, preparing ourselves to do what we expect to do, rather than vainly trying to produce polished 'all rounders'.

This discipline revealed one basic need common to each man, a systematic, working knowledge of the Bible. We were more concerned about the content of Scripture and its practical application, than the niceties of critical scholarship. We hope to store this knowledge in

such a way that it will readily be available when needed. We believe
that much of this understanding can best be acquired by a process of
discovery, starting with our experience of the world about us, and
proceeding to the Bible's teaching relating to that situation. We are
wary of the idea that one lecture on each book of the Bible will give
us what we need to know; we prefer to look for principles which will
help us to go to the Bible to find what we need when we need it.
Rather than a conducted tour of the house, we are looking for a key
which will let us into the house: the ability to think biblically and the
instinct which will help us to apply this to life.

Much of this study is done informally in the group. We have also
benefitted greatly from the ministry of teachers who have spent
occasional evenings with us. Each man is committed to a three year
plan by which he will become acquainted with the whole of the Bible
by reading a chapter each day. We are also working on a 'panorama'
of the Bible which will help us to discover the broad themes of
Scripture. Each man has selected two or three books, from both Old
and New Testament, which he intends to study in depth during the
next three years. We hope to acquire skill in handling the Bible by
learning such principles as the purpose of parables and how to understand them, the nature and purpose of Biblical symbols, the significance
and interpretation of prophecy, and the meaning and purpose of
poetry.

Other subjects which will need attention during the course are
personal spiritual discipline, worship, pastoralia, doctrine, pastoral
counselling and teaching methods. We have spent a year on Church
History during which we read Roger Lloyd's History of the Church
of England 1900–1965, and all the men spent two terms on the study
of small group behaviour.

Each year is divided into three terms of ten weeks, in which we
expect to spend one evening each week on personal study and one in a
seminar. The bishop comes once a term, and on those evenings the
wives join us. Between terms, more time is available for the practical
work in the church to which each man is committed. We are all
encouraged to regard this regular service, together with everyday
experience at work and at home, as further opportunity to learn.

We also try to share with each other the lessons we are learning. Experiences are often discussed in the group, and are also written up in a personal log which is regularly submitted to the vicar for comment. The vicar, in turn, circulates his log to all the members of the group. We find that there are many learning situations naturally available: day conferences, outside engagements shared with staff members, and two week-ends away together each year. One week-end spent with members of the Southwark Ordination Course was particularly valuable.

We have tried to give attention to the needs of our wives by involving them in week-ends and some of the evening seminars. Living near each other and sharing the same church life, it is possible to share experiences. Our aim has been to encourage a natural partnership between husband and wife, rather than to regard the wives as a collective force of potential labour; they do not therefore tend to meet as a separate group, although they have done so on occasion.

The aspects of training which we have found most valuable are probably those which are most difficult to describe. It is an advantage to have the vicar as personal tutor and pastor, available to spend unhurried time sharing problems and dealing with questions which arise at points of growth. The fellowship within the group itself has become an increasing strength. The realization is dawning that 'every situation is a learning situation', and this engenders a sense of excitement. Confidence is growing as we discover new skills and gifts in each other and, above all, realize that one does not have to pass exams to be an effective minister. We have discovered that training can be effective without being academic; that apprenticeship is as valid here as anywhere; that hard work can be fun.

Concentration upon learning by experience is obviously likely to create problems which we have yet to discover. We are still liable to impose our preconceived ideas of what the ministry should be, but some new attitudes have emerged. The danger of losing touch with reality is still with us; the group of friends has become very important to us and does sometimes seem more important to us than the world around. We believe, however, that close identity with a small group of equals does prevent us from getting too many false ideas of ourselves and of the task before us. Perhaps there is less temptation to indulge in fantasies about the future than there is in a traditional training situation.

The strengths of this method seem to us to be that the men who have little educational qualification are on an equal footing with those who have more. Ideally, the whole of life is potential training. If we master that principle, the men will continue to grow after the period of formal training is complete. The training is a gradual process; the men take increasing responsibility by degrees, pastorally and by way of baptism interviews, leading services, preaching and so on. Since working class men prefer practical experience to theoretical teaching, the method suits our culture.

I was asked by the bishop to produce a mid-course assessment of our programme. A few quotations from my notes may help to illustrate what has been said about our attempt at practical training.

'The essential relationship between priesthood and self denial is kept before us constantly. Instead of one big question, e.g. "Do I offer myself for the ministry and go to college?" we face questions like, "Does the TV, my tiredness, my right to rest have first claim *tonight*?"

'Training in the context of everyday work and the neighbourhood situation keeps certain facts before us which could be avoided more easily in a residential college. First, the fact that sharing openly in Christ's ministry means making yourself vulnerable to others. Secondly the cost of being natural—e.g. for a working class man, the pain of expressing emotion—and the value of familiar friends constantly at hand to check our tendency to assume unnatural attitudes. Living in the situation towards which we are working helps us to avoid the tendency to indulge in fantasies of what "being a minister" will be like.

'We have always hoped that our method would enable us to involve our wives in the training more readily than is possible in a residential situation. In practice it is still very difficult, and depends a great deal on an individual's willingness to relive situations for the sake of sharing them with his wife. In principle, there is obviously a greater degree of joint growth than there would be if the man were away from home.'

(v) A specific term of service

The Supplementary Ministers have accepted that they will be licensed to officiate for seven years. When the time comes for licences to be renewed, the bishop will decide whether or not to do so after consulting the men, the vicar and the PCCs. This decision was taken for two reasons.

(a) to encourage a flow of leadership

The four men range in age from 30 to 60. Even so, it is not difficult to imagine what would happen if they were all allowed to grow old together. Their authority would become unchallengeable, they could easily begin to impose increasingly conservative attitudes upon the churches, and they would be like a 'blood clot' blocking the flow of new young leadership.

Most churches have known a similar experience. Churchwardens often become so firmly established in office over a number of years, that it becomes unthinkable to replace them even though they may have become dictatorial or worse. To create a leadership group is to risk creating a power group. For the sake of the men themselves, as well as for the churches, it was agreed that we should take precautions now to avoid an evil which, however unlikely it may seem at the moment, is certainly a possibility.

(b) to challenge a traditional attitude

For some men the call of God to the ministry is unmistakably a call for life. They are certain from the moment of ordination that they are happy to spend the rest of their working lives in a parish ministry. Others do not have the same confidence, and therefore hesitate about ordination. Some find that after having been ordained for some years they want to withdraw from work in a parish. Tradition suggests that to do so would be a failure.

Because the whole pattern of Supplementary Ministry is so unconventional and its future development so uncertain, we decided that it would be wrong for our men to accept this tradition of lifetime commitment without question. They needed to be free to withdraw if God so guided, without feeling that they were spiritually, or in some other way, inferior.

It may well be that there are many men who would be set free to offer valuable service in the ministry if it were once established that they could do so without binding themselves to a certain way of life far into the unseen future.

This decision need not beg the vexed question of the indelibility of orders. Once accept that the status of priesthood may be separated from its function, and it becomes possible to hold the status of priest for life without having to exercise the function in any conventional sense. Indeed, as society becomes more mobile, it may well be that many men will want to take up and put down the function of priesthood several times during their working life, and then exercise it in quite a different way again after retirement.

It was accepted by the full time staff at the time this decision was made that their appointments would be subject to a similar review.

(vi) Voluntary service

Since the word 'voluntary' has two distinct meanings, it would be wise to separate them. A volunteer undertakes certain duties of his own free will as opposed to the conscript who has no choice. During the last war there was a difference between the volunteer who chose to join the services, and the conscript who was called up and had to go or break the law. The word is also used to speak of those who give their labour free of charge, as opposed to those who are paid. In this sense we attach no value judgment to the term. For very good reasons some are paid. For equally good reasons volunteers are not. It is in this latter sense that the word is used here.

All Christian workers are volunteers in the first sense of the word, but not in the second. There is certainly nothing original about voluntary ministry; much effective work has been done by those who have received no salary. But the idea is still regarded as a departure from the norm. In working class communities there are particularly strong arguments in favour of ministers not being paid. It would be impossible to argue this case without reference to Roland Allen. In 1930 he wrote the last of his prophetic books, *The Case for Voluntary Clergy*. Copies are now very scarce, but his main arguments may be found in an anthology edited by D. M. Paton.[11]

Allen's experience on the mission field created a burning conviction which he spent his life arguing—that Christians had imposed their own preconceptions upon the churches overseas, rather than encouraging, as Paul did, the natural growth of indigenous churches. The results we know too well: a string of missions which reflect the attitudes and culture of western Christians. Because they are alien they do not grow spontaneously. They depend for their support upon further doses of that which caused the original sickness, foreign aid. The vicious circle is complete. What Allen could not know was that Britain was to become, in our day, a mission field. The reason his books are now beginning to be read so widely is that all he said applies to us now, as much as ever it did to the mission churches overseas.

Allen argued that we frustrate the growth of indigenous churches and perpetuate the alien mission tradition by almost everything we do. Our educational principles, our attitudes to finance, the discouragement of self government, the failure to encourage local initiative and spontaneous growth, have all been working against biblical missionary principles. We have been more concerned to reproduce churches which conform to patterns with which we are familiar, than to follow New Testament missionary principles of spontaneous church growth. Nearly all his arguments can be applied almost word for word to the situation in the vast urban industrial areas of England. Christians have been more concerned to reproduce the patterns of church life which are familiar in the middle class areas in which the church is traditionally strongest. Since the clergy are drawn from the middle classes, this is hardly surprising. Those ministers who are recruited from the working class soon become absorbed into the prevailing middle class tradition.

Allen argues that it is essential to recruit voluntary clergy if indigenous churches are to be established, not only because finance demands it, but, even more important, because only in this way will the particular evil be overcome, which he described in the words of Mandell Creighton: 'The Church is divided into two bodies, one offering, the other accepting Christian privileges'.[12]

By our established traditions we have identified vocation to the service of God with the vocation to join a profession. This identification causes needless and sinful confusion. We may not believe in that identification, but because we pay the clergy, anyone not directly committed to the system sees it in that way. Allen quotes the example of a man who was actually ordained as a voluntary curate at a stipend of £1 per year! He did not want a substantial salary, so he was paid an illusory one. Rather than admit to the principle of voluntary clergy, the church had to bring this man into the stipendiary order; he must be made to join the profession as a professional. The very smallness of the salary gives emphasis to its importance.

Forty years on, it may seem that Allen presses his argument too hard. We are familiar with unpaid clergymen in principle. But the fact remains that as recently as 1956 John Osborne wrote: 'During the past fifty years, the church has repeatedly ducked every moral issue that has been thrown at its head—poverty, unemployment, Fascism, war, South Africa, the H-bomb, and so on. It has lived in an atmosphere of calm, casual funk. It has not been entirely negative in its attitude. It has even managed to spread the gospel of funk. With its village quarrels about divorce and remarriage, and its favourite topic—the reimbursement of the clergy—its capacity for self-mockery has been unlimited.'[13]

Anyone with experience of working class attitudes will agree that the confusion of vocation and profession has led many people to under-value the sacrifice of some full time ministers simply because they are paid. The effect of the confusion can be observed both outside and inside the church.

Those outside the church can treat anything said or done by professional clergymen as suspect. However sacrificial an action may be or however genuine an intention as an expression of the love of Christ, it is always possible to respond with, 'Well, he's paid to do it'. However true and convincing the word of God may be in the experience of the speaker, it is always possible to answer, 'Well, he's got to say that, it's his job'. A voluntary clergyman is free from that suspicion.

Those inside the church have been bred in the tradition described by Mandell Creighton: two bodies, 'one offering, the other accepting Christian privileges'. Generations of paternalistic clergy have fostered acquiescence among Christians in areas like East London. While there is a professional at hand to bear the responsibility for the life and health of the local church, there will be Christians who will say, 'That's what he's there for'.

There is no guarantee that voluntary clergy will avoid being tarred with the same brush, but doing without a salary may help to avoid the danger. At least it will be impossible for anyone to say, 'They are paid to do it'. Perhaps our team will make some progress towards correcting the idea that the church may be divided into 'givers' and 'receivers'. Our hope is that by discovering the joy of service, through their partnership in ministry, they will then be able to spread the idea that service is a joyful privilege, to be given freely, not labour to be rewarded.

3 New Testament Authority

An indigenous church is needed in East London. An indigenous church demands an indigenous ministry. But these six arguments for supplementary ministry would be meaningless if this pattern did not have New Testament authority. In fact the Biblical picture suggests 'varieties of ministries'. Our traditional concept is much more settled, rigid and inflexible than anything found in the New Testament. The security of an unchangeable order of ordained ministry, laid down once for all in the early church, arises from a misreading of history. True, there was an itinerant ministry in the New Testament. Some of these mobile ministers were paid by the church, but some of them earned their own living. Certainly the local church could never have regarded those who came in temporarily from outside as 'the Ministry', as we have come to do. It was normal for the local church to produce its own ministry from within its own membership. It seems to be high time we returned to apostolic practice.

This particular plan has emerged as an attempt to meet our need in East London. I am not qualified to judge how valid it would be elsewhere. I have often wondered, for example, if some form of Supplementary Ministry would help to meet the needs of the church in rural areas. If the principles are sound they should be adaptable to any situation. We shall now test the soundness of the principles against some of the arguments which are presented against the scheme.

Notes to Chapter 3

[1] Bishop E. R. Wickham, in a private document.
[2] Charles Booth: The Life and Labour of the people of London 1890–1900 (Macmillan, 1902).
[3] Peter Willmott and Michael Young: Family and Kinship in East London (Pelican, 1957) page 93.
[4] Richard Hoggart: The Uses of Literacy (Pelican, 1957).
[5] The Observer, February 11 1962.
[6] Affluence and the British Class Structure, Sociological Review, Vol. II no 2 New Series, July 1963.
[7] The Sociology of Modern Britain, ed. Butterworth and Weir (Fontana, 1970) pages 209–212.
[8] The Guardian, February 15 1972.
[9] Bishop E. R. Wickham, in a private document.
[10] Abbé Michonneau, Revolution in a City Parish (Blackfriars) page 63.
[11] D. M. Paton, The Ministry of the Spirit (World Dominion Press, 1960).
[12] Mrs Creighton, Life and Letters, vol II, page 375.
[13] John Osborne, Declaration, page 74.

4 The Difficulties

Some of the greatest difficulties we have experienced, as we have tried to work out in practice a plan for indigenous ministry, have come from within our own fellowship. Tensions have been created, as we have tried to understand the effect of these changes upon our churches. Painful conflicts of personal relationships could not be avoided, and resolving them has often been costly. These difficulties are part of the price which must be paid for any new initiative within an established institution. Sometimes our determination to persevere has been sorely tested, we have had to ask ourselves if the final object-ive justifies the effort.

We have also had to answer many objections from outside our own churches, but as we examined them we found that none we have heard so far are really objections; they are difficulties. There is a vital difference between an objection and a difficulty. If a valid objection to the princi-ple is sustained, we must abandon the principle. A difficulty is con-cerned with the practice, it does not challenge the basic principle. There are a number of complex legal and organizational problems to be faced. Once one is convinced that the creation of an indigenous ministry is God's will for the church in its present need, these problems cease to be barriers in the way of action. They are simply difficulties to be overcome.

Many difficulties arise from the attitude of some existing full time ministers. Effective part time ministry demands a willingness to welcome a new type of priest as a genuine partner. No one should imagine that it will be easy. The process of adjustment raises funda-mental spiritual and practical questions which most of us would prefer to leave buried. The effectiveness of the ministry, even the health of

49

the church, demands that we dig up those buried questions and examine them.

We need to help each other see whether the difficulties we raise are the result of that instinct which resists change. Action often provokes reaction. The only motive force capable of overcoming such instinctive reaction is the conviction that the principle of an indigenous ministry is biblical and a valid step towards the creation of an indigenous church.

In order to see Supplementary Ministry in its proper light, we need to recapture the idea of the church as a living society. In East London a church is likely to be a small group. Led by voluntary clergy with a full time minister as resource man, these small groups are going to discover important truths. They are going to find that, as in the tragic death of the baby during our training programme, the whole church is involved and not just the clergyman. They are going to find a new sense of identity. They are going to be a body, with their own leaders, called to lead a distinctive life, a Christian life. With leaders involved in the demands of everyday life just like their neighbours, these groups will more readily discover the points of need in their neighbourhood. It will be harder, but not impossible, to avoid the demands to serve the community than it is in the larger group led by a professional clergyman cushioned from society, particularly working class society, by stipend, vicarage and the maintenance of the church 'machine'.

It is the intention of our team of voluntary clergy, in partnership with the full time staff, to challenge that terrible division of the church into two groups, and encourage the creation of a living society. If we only add to the number of clergymen offering religious privileges to a group who are content to receive them, we shall have done the opposite of what we intend. Even if we add numbers to our churches, if those congregations remain simply loose affiliations of like minded people who disperse the moment the service is ended, we shall only have succeeded in perpetuating that which we set out to correct, and the last state will be worse than the first.

This objective, a living Christian community, is implicit in the answers to the ten difficulties we have so far heard. It is particularly relevant to the first, which is the one we take most seriously.

1 Why ordination?

This question was put most persistently, if not too picturesquely, by one bishop in these terms, 'What happens to lay involvement if you slap a dog-collar on all your best men?'

I have no intention of treating a serious question flippantly when I ask whether the use of 'dog-collar' in the bishop's question does not reflect a hidden notion of the ministry. A group of men in dog-collars, behaving as men in dog-collars are expected to do, would certainly perpetuate the 'terrible division'. More men officially recognized—and dressed—to administer Christian privileges, would almost certainly strengthen the assumption of the remainder that their only responsibility was meekly to receive what was offered. A proper lay involvement would certainly be stifled.

If the use of the 'dog-collar' metaphor does in fact symbolize this subconscious objection, it is proper to answer symbolically. From the outset we knew that we would have to give serious thought to the question of what clothes our men would wear after their ordination. For some time we pushed the problem to the back of our minds, assuming that it was not urgent and could be dealt with later. Eventually we became convinced that the decision *was* important, not so much for itself as for what it represented. The distinctive dress they wore would reflect the men's own idea of themselves. Were they to be copies of the existing model, aping the traditional full time minister, or were they to demonstrate the fact that they saw themselves reflecting a different attitude, by refusing even to look like a conventional clergyman?

We spent the best part of one of our week-ends away discussing the subject, and found it very hard indeed to make a firm decision. At the moment it looks as though they would feel bound to wear cassock, surplice and scarf for the Holy Communion, at least for the time being. They would prefer not to wear anything distinctive in church at other times. They certainly have no intention of wearing dog-collars! We do not want to perpetuate a traditional view of clergy as the 'givers'. We do not even want to create a new pattern, so much as to return to what we believe to be the original pattern

In New Testament terms God gave a variety of gifts for a variety of ministries: 'some to be apostles ... some pastors and teachers, to equip God's people for work in His service' (Ephesians 4.11-12, NEB).

In these terms the minister is clearly not to be designated God's official servant while the rest of the church is served, but 'to equip God's people for work in His service'. That is, to be the one chosen to enable *the whole church* to be God's servant; to set the church free to be itself.

Canon Douglas Webster comments on this scripture: 'The ordained ministry may be said to exist primarily for the church, enabling the church to fulfil its much wider and fuller ministry in the world ... we may therefore say that the ministry is God's gift to the church, and the church is God's gift to the world, His agent for mission.'[1]

In the early days of our scheme one of the men answered the question 'why ordination?' with another question, 'why not?' This is not the superficial reply it may, at first sight, appear, if the argument for an indigenous church in East London is accepted. One of the greatest obstacles to the establishment of an indigenous church is rooted in the local church itself. The effects of generations of well meant but stultifying paternalism need to be overcome A sense of confidence needs to be generated among working class Christians that they are genuinely respected. The fact must be established that those from outside, who in the past have done all the leading, do actually believe that a locally-rooted responsible Christian church can be established in these areas. The church as at present organized places great store by ordination. Working class Christians would believe that they were being given their due respect once a genuinely working class ministry had been established. If local Christians are to be given confidence to explore and use the gifts given them by God and peculiar to their culture, their share of local leadership must be, and must be seen to be, nothing less than full partnership.

The concept of a 'working class church' must naturally be questioned. It has already been argued (on pages 21-27) that divisions exist and cannot be ignored. Nevertheless it must be admitted that those divisions are sinful and impoverish each group which is allowed to develop in isolation from others. Unfortunately, working class culture and the valuable contribution it should be making to the fullness of 'life in Christ' cannot flourish while the church continues to be dominated by middle class attitudes. Something like a 'working class church' must be allowed to emerge before working class Christians can become sufficiently sure of themselves, and of the value of what they have to offer, to be able to make their contribution to the whole church on anything like an equal footing.

Black Power emerged in the United States because black people were forced into ghettoes and told they were inferior. Now that white people want to integrate, the blacks are saying they are going to stay where they have been put until they have made their ghettoes as least as good as the rest of society. When they have the best schools, the best housing, a fair deal, in short when the white man has accepted that black is beautiful, then the blacks will come out and integrate.

Black Power is regrettable; a working class church is certainly not desirable. But the same logic applies to both. They are both a reasonable response to those attitudes which want to put one section of society into a ghetto and regard it as inferior. Those who want to see an indigenous church in East London long to achieve their dream without conflict. We believe that the strong and distinctive working class contribution which will eventually emerge will be for the benefit of the whole church, and to the glory of God.

In the end, the crucial question 'why ordination?' is not a question about ordination but about whether we believe that a locally-rooted responsible Christian church can be established in the huge one-class areas of our industrial cities.

2 'Ordination on the cheap'

The reaction of those who fear that Supplementary Ministry will result in a lowering of standards is understandable, but is based on the inherited attitudes already examined, and is false for three reasons.

(i) *because academic ability is not the only valid yardstick*
Those who are fearful of lowered standards are usually thinking of academic standards, not personal qualifications for ministry. Academic

ability is not the only, or necessarily the best, test of a man's intelligence; provided there is an 'academic man' available when needed, we want *intelligent* men as ministers.

The leaders of a local church must be able to handle ideas; we do not want dull men as priests. But academic achievement and intelligence are not the same thing. In the Robbins Report (1960–61) one table divided children into three ability bands and related ability to examination success. This showed that children of professional parents did better than children of working class parents. That may not seem surprising. What is remarkable is the fact that 'professional' children in the lowest ability band were likely to become better 'O' level candidates than working class children in the top ability band. While ordination is geared to examination success there is an inevitable bias in favour of the middle class candidate. A working class man, because he has not a natural aptitude for academic work, is being improperly excluded from the ministry. The argument then becomes, not 'are we asking for ordination on the cheap?' but 'is ordination, for the working man, too expensive—even priced in the wrong currency?'

The fact that a man cannot pass exams does not mean that he has not got the intelligence required of a minister. Basil Bernstein[2] has shown the close connection between social class and the use of language. Middle class children are encouraged to use a much more elaborate code of language than the children of working class parents. If a child is only able to use a restricted code, he will only be able to achieve a limited verbal reasoning score, with the result that he will be written down as less intelligent than he is. That will remain with him as a birthright even though it is based upon false assumptions. Intelligence is not a place upon a ladder on which everyone is allotted a particular rung. Rather we should try to think in terms of a series of ladders called intelligenc*es*. Each of us has a different place on each of these ladders. Many working class men who would be low down on the ladder of academic intelligence may well be high up the ladder of intelligence which is judged on ability to think creatively, interpret situations or understand the needs of others. Ways must be found to recognize and harness each kind of intelligence. Every kind is needed in the ministry.

(ii) what is cheap by one standard may be expensive by another
We are all familiar with the idea that a doctor, teacher or lawyer may be ordained with a minimum of training, in some cases with no training at all. Those professional men who are required to work at the exams do not find the demands too great, because they are used to books and can reach the required standard without too much difficulty.

When I compare the five years of hard work being asked of our four men with the three years I spent at Theological College, I am again forced to ask, 'What do we mean by cheap?' If anyone paid a price during my training, it was my wife, not me. Once the costly decision had been made to accept the claims of the ministry, life was very pleasant for me. She had to stay at home alone and earn a living. My grants paid for a very comfortable life, stimulating work and congenial company. The three years went very quickly. Our men are being asked to give up the rightful claim to a large part of their free time, to work late into the night and accept a discipline which is even more demanding because it is lived out at home and not enforced by life in a community.

(iii) cheapness assumes something being bought
It is hard to avoid the conclusion that the fear of 'ordination on the cheap' springs from the idea of professionalism mentioned earlier. Our inherited concept of the ministry assumes that to enter the ministry is to enter one of the professions. If ordination is the qualification whereby a man is to earn a living, then it follows that he must achieve the minimum standards required by the profession. A doctor must 'qualify' before being registered; a solicitor must serve his articles before he is admitted; a clergyman must pass GOE before being ordained. Given the assumption that something of material gain is to follow from admission to the profession, a basic qualification is essential. There will always be justification for high professional standards being required of professional clergy.

But it has already been argued that Supplementary Ministers do not want to earn their living from the ministry. They are not wanting to buy a right to earn a living; so how can they be said to want it 'on the cheap'? They are wanting the opportunity to serve God in a particular way, as they would want to protect the right of full time ministers to serve God in their way. That privilege is surely given by God and cannot be bought, cheaply or otherwise.

3 What happens if they move?

One of the fundamental concepts of our scheme is the fact that the men are ordained to a local ministry. They have been called by the local church to serve in that church. It is right therefore to ask what will happen if for personal reasons the men move to another part of the country. The church in their new parish may not welcome their ministry. The incumbent may not need their help or accept the principle of partnership. The bishop may not be satisfied with their qualifications. They may find themselves in a middle class district where their working class insights no longer apply.

We have always realized that this could happen, and the men accept that their right to officiate in any church will depend completely upon their being acceptable to the local church. That will be true whether they move or not. Again, it is interesting to trace one of the assumptions about the existing ministry reflected in this question. Ordination has always implied that the clergyman will continue to function as a clergyman for the rest of his life. This is not essential.

Expectations can change over the years, however. It could be that after several years of personally satisfying ministry a man may not readily accept that his ministry would not be welcome in a new situation. If this should happen, the present system of licensing should be adequate safeguard against the unpleasantness which might otherwise arise. The bishop is at liberty to grant or withhold a license depending upon his own and the local church's view of their needs at the time.

4 What happens if they are offered livings?

Common sense demands recognition of the fact that human beings are not always consistent. While the men may all say now that they have no intention of earning their living in the ministry, attitudes can change over the years. What is to stop them from accepting sole charge of a parish for which they may well not be fitted?

The Welsby Report[3] proposed that all men—not only those ordained to an auxiliary pastoral ministry—should go through one process of selection, training and ordination. If at a later date any of them wanted to be considered for sole charge of a cure of souls, they should then go through a further process of selection. This is a sound suggestion in its own right. It would also be an effective safeguard against this possible weakness in Supplementary Ministry.

It may well be that one or more of the Supplementary Ministers will prove himself well qualified for sole charge, in which case we would want to argue that this proposal be instituted to make it possible for such a man to be admitted to a living, as much as to keep the wrong men out.

5 Once a priest always a priest

A man ordained as a Supplementary Minister must be prepared to accept limitations upon the exercise of his ministry (see 3 above). Those who believe that a priest's orders are indelible have sometimes assumed that this practice would challenge the principle of indelibility.

Once again we need to separate the principle from the fixed ideas of ministry which we have inherited. We have always believed that once ordained, a clergyman will function as a clergyman for the rest of his life. Generally speaking, if he does move out of parish work it will be into school teaching or some similar profession, where he can still be identified as a clergyman. It is comparatively rare for a clergyman to cease functioning as a clergyman. Rare but not unknown. In those cases known to me, it has never been suggested that the man who ceases to function as a clergyman surrenders his status as a priest. It is accepted that if such a man decided to offer himself again for ministry, he would be perfectly justified in doing so. No question of re-ordination would be suggested.

All we are proposing is that, after a man is ordained, it should not be taken for granted that he will thereafter for ever hold office as a licensed minister. It is perfectly possible to put down the office without having to surrender the status of a priest.

This view would seem to be reflected by the *Form of Ordaining of Priests* in the Book of Common Prayer. The bishop is required to say to the newly ordained priest: 'Take thou authority to preach the Word of God, and to minister the holy Sacraments in the Congregation, *where thou shalt be lawfully appointed thereunto.*'

This does not convey authority to officiate anywhere. It assumes the need for a licence to convey 'lawful appointment'. Licence and priesthood are certainly not the same thing. 'Once a priest always a priest' does not assume 'once a priest, always a right to officiate'. Indelibility only argues that a man can only be ordained once. He can no more be reordained than he can be rebaptized. Licence to officiate has always been a completely separate issue. It is local and temporary, 'where thou shalt be lawfully appointed.'

6 Why priest's orders?

One of the basic arguments for an indigenous ministry rests upon the need to convince working class Christians that they are trusted and respected. People who have grown used to the idea that they are the ones to be led, rather than the leaders, need to be convinced of their value. It will have to be established that their contribution is essential to the creation of a genuine locally rooted church. Ordination will give that confidence. But it must therefore be 'the real thing'. An order of eldership or a permanent diaconate would be quite adequate. The men would be qualified to perform the duties required of them. But, given this symbolic function of ordination, adequacy is not enough. At all costs we must avoid the danger of creating a second class ministry. Nothing less than full partnership will do, if genuine local initiative is to thrive.

In addition to the need to encourage local confidence, there is also a great need to correct the heritage of the past. For a working class man, much of what happens to him encourages him to think of himself as second class. The job he does, the place he lives in, the school he goes to and so on, all speak much more loudly than words. They say that 'middle class is better'. For generations the church in East London has been, often unwittingly, preaching this gospel. The unspoken assumption has been that the church is here as the agency of the middle classes, to help to improve you—that is, make you middle class; your job is to receive what is being given, gratefully and respectfully. The time has come to repent of this arrogance, to accept a learner's place. Middle class 'outsiders' must realize that they offer help when needed; they do not exercise authority as of right. In the circumstances, to suggest anything less than priest's orders would be to perpetuate the evil attitudes of the past, and do more harm than good.

7 What happens when a new vicar comes?

If we do succeed in establishing a strong and effective local leadership, how can we guarantee that they will get on with the next incumbent?

Many of the questions at issue in the church at present are closely related. Once you begin to think about patterns of ministry, you find yourself asking questions about patronage!

I cannot resist pointing out yet again how this frequently asked question reflects the way in which the church is at present organized in favour of the clergy. The question is almost always asked in this form. It takes for granted the fact that it is the responsibility of the men to get on with the new incumbent. If we were not so clergy-centred in our attitudes, we would realize that it is the business of the incumbent to adapt to the needs of the local situation. Surely, the question should be expressed the other way: How can we guarantee that the next incumbent will get on with the team of Supplementary Ministers?

If, after several years of hard work and careful consultation with the congregations, a principle has been established which is accepted and thought to be important, some way must be found to ensure that the views of a prospective incumbent and the existing team of local ministers can be seen to agree, before the new man is appointed.

Rather than a disadvantage, we see genuine benefit arising from the existence of a team of local ministers during the vacancy of a living. Apart from the fact that they will be able to combat the notion that

everything must await the new incumbent, they will be able to ensure
continuity. Often an important policy is not carried on to the point
where it becomes most effective, because there is no satisfactory way
of passing on thinking from one incumbent to the next. The Rev.
Peter Yacomeni found that the team of elders which existed at St
Luke Barton Hill when he was appointed, was able to be his
teacher!

We do not assume that the incumbent will always be the leader
of the team. It may well be that, in time, the job would be done better
by one of the Supplementary Ministers, enabling the full time college
trained man to exercise a more effective 'enabling' ministry.

It is also possible that in due course one of the Supplementary
Ministers will qualify for appointment to a living and become the
incumbent.

Neither of these questions can be anything more than theory at
this point in time, but we would like to keep the options open.

8 Won't you have to revise the Ordinal?

The only part of the form of Ordering of Priests which seems to me to
pose any problems for Supplementary Ministry is the exhortation
where the bishop says: 'Ye ought to forsake and set aside (as much as
you may) all wordly cares and studies. We have good hope that you
have well weighed and pondered these things with yourselves long
before this time; and that you have clearly determined, by God's
grace, to give yourselves wholly to this office, whereunto it has
pleased God to call you; so that, as much as lieth in you, you will
apply yourselves wholly to this one thing, and draw all your cares
and studies this way.'

There are two phrases here which seem to contradict the principles
of Supplementary Ministry:

(i) 'Ye ought to forsake and set aside . . . all wordly cares and studies.'
Traditionally we have taken these words to mean that a man ordained
priest must earn his living by means of a clerical stipend, not an
everyday job. Again, we assume this because it is the pattern to which we

are accustomed. It is not the New Testament pattern. This exhortation bears strong resemblance to Paul's last exhortation to the Ephesian elders (Acts 20.18–35). But the Ephesian elders were voluntary clergy. Paul ends this address to them by saying that they ought to labour with their hands, both to earn their own living and to have the means to help those in need (Acts 20.35). Rather than arguing that they should be supported by the church, he encouraged them to supply the needs of the church themselves.

We are so used to thinking of these words in terms of leaving the hurly burly of the market place for the seclusion and separation of a clerical income, that we cannot think of them in any other way. But they could not be obeyed by a mere forsaking of wordly business. The spirit of these words demands more than the giving up of a means of livelihood. A priest should always remember his priestly duties and put them first in his life. Surely a Supplementary Minister is going to accept that claim as readily as any other? The words do not mean any less if the priest is earning his living in a secular job, than if he is expecting to be maintained by the church. They do not mean less because they do not mean, 'forsake the ordinary cares of men and then you will be free to serve God'. They may even mean more. Obedience to these words is internal, not external; and the internal is not less than the external, but more.

(ii) *'You will apply yourself wholly to this one thing and draw all your cares and studies this way.'*

Again it is in keeping with our traditional assumptions that we should take 'studies' in this case to mean the study of books. It is equally valid to apply the word to the study of life. A Supplementary Minister will be just as able to draw all his study of life towards the exercise of his priesthood.

The words are calling the ordinand to remember that he is a priest in all his daily business; doing his daily work as a man of God should do it. He is being warned that if he acts in his daily work unworthily, the priesthood, the church and the name of Christ will be brought into discredit. That is no less true of a Supplementary Minister than it is of any other priest.

The exhortation is telling every priest that he must not let wordly cares hinder him from his spiritual duty. He must never forget that he is a priest, whatever work he may be doing. That is true whether the man earns his living with his hands, in a profession or from a clerical stipend. To say that it means simply, 'Give up all involvement in wordly affairs so far as your income is concerned and separate yourself from the laity by doing a different kind of job' is to make it mean less, not more.

9 Won't we be flooded with clergy?

This is a curious argument at a time when the church is constantly concerned about the shortage of men for the ministry. But the question has been asked and needs to be answered.

In the particular circumstances we have in mind, there are so few working class Christians deeply committed to the church that there would, in the foreseeable future, be too few suitable candidates rather than too many. In that sense, this scheme calls for an act of faith if it is to be anything more than an experiment in one place. We have to begin somewhere. There is cause for hope that God intends to change the pattern of defeat in urban areas. It is our duty to act on that assumption.

Elsewhere in the country there may well be many more men who would want to offer themselves for ordination. The army of loyal Readers may well begin to ask why they should not have their ministry regularized by becoming Supplementary Ministers. Some will argue that this will result in a flood of unsuitable candidates. That may or may not be true; it will be the responsibility of the whole church to ensure that only suitable candidates are ordained.

We have been asked why there are no women in our team. The answer is that we thought it best not to add to the problems we already had. The questions we have raised in our attempt to create a working class ministry would have become needlessly complicated if we had added the different set of questions which are raised by women's ministry. By facing both problems at once we would have created confusion and risked getting the wrong answers on both counts.

If this present plan succeeds and we decide to start a second group, this would almost certainly contain some women. First, because there are so many able women in our parishes whose ministry would be strengthened by being regularized. Second, because Supplementary Ministry provides a convenient vehicle for demonstrating that the objections to women's ministry are emotional, not theological.

The church may well grow weaker still for lack of clergy. It is unlikely that an abundance will have the same effect. The disease may cause some inconvenience; it is unlikely to be fatal.

This is one area in which we have to admit a possible danger without being certain what the future might bring. Times of advance are always times of greatest danger. If the Holy Spirit is prompting us to take a step forward, it is unwise, to say the least, to ask that we should know in detail where that step will take us.

10 Is a working class man a suitable candidate for the ministry?

This last objection is seldom if ever openly stated. The fact that it is hidden and unadmitted makes it the more difficult to answer. Most of us would deny that we entertain such disreputable thoughts, but the fact remains that while we readily accept the suitability of a lawyer or accountant, we have misgivings about the fitness of a docker or building worker as a candidate for the ministry.

Roland Allen quotes the Rev. E. Hill describing a catechist named Josiah Ngcombu. 'He says that "this man . . . in all his actions made me realize that I had a subordinate in office, but a superior as a man to work under me . . . He had been converted somewhere in Zululand or Natal, and had eventually made his way along the Cape Government Railway and become boss boy in the big coal shed at Norval's Point. There he lived with his wife and held services regularly for natives . . . He prepared men and women for Baptism, and Christians for confirmation. He was asked by Mr Douglas Ellison, of the Railway Mission, to give up his lucrative billet as boss boy of the coal shed and to come to Naavwpoort for a greatly reduced salary as catechist. He readily consented, and when I once asked him if he regretted the change and loss of money he merely said, 'No, boss; I get more time for prayer now.' . . . Josiah never lost his influence over his flock, and the candidates he asked me to examine for baptism and confirmation always astonished me . . . I never remember him losing a single communicant. He was a shepherd who led them, and sought them out and never failed to watch."

'Naturally this man was not ordained. He is a typical example of the man whom we do not ordain. He had all the qualifications demanded by the Apostle; but not all the qualifications which we demand.'

There are men like this in English working class parishes today. They are not yet ordained. We still demand the wrong qualifications.

A bishop recently told me that professional candidates are beginning to present themselves for Auxiliary Pastoral Ministry from the suburban end of his diocese. There had been no problem accepting them. The difficulty would come when the first labourer presented himself from the inner city district at the other end of the diocese.

The attitude which discriminates between 'suitable' occupations has certainly existed, and no doubt it will continue. It hardly becomes the Church of Christ, whose chief apostles were fishermen. The point was made by Canon Douglas Webster in his report on part time ministry in South America. He was sent on behalf of CMS to study the phenomenon of voluntary ministry in the churches there. He discovered that where the minister of a church was not full time, the local Christians had pronounced opinions about the sort of job from which a minister should earn his living. 'It was felt that there must be compatibility between the ministry and the secular job chosen. The professions were singled out in preference to industry. With one group I was tempted—in the manner of Abraham's prayer for Sodom—to lead them down the social and status scale, in order to discover how far down compatibility reached. I asked finally, "Would a minister be acceptable if he were a carpenter?" Without a moment's thought the answer given was, "No".'[4]

Perhaps it would help to put all these difficulties in perspective if we reversed roles. Instead of pleading for a return to what I believe to be a New Testament pattern: varieties of ministry, let us imagine the effect upon a Christian familiar with the Apostolic practice of the suggestion to introduce our present system.

'You intend to put one man in charge of a parish by himself?' he would ask. 'How could one man possibly survive the pressures alone? Do you really believe that there is one man who has all the gifts?'

'So you want to send us a man we have never met? The idea makes us anxious; we prefer to choose men from among our own number who have proved themselves. You may argue that your man has capability, but we are more interested in proved capacity.'

'The man you want to send us is a foreigner. It will be years before he understands us well enough to do what our men can do instinctively. Let him come as one of our team, by all means. We shall welcome and respect him as a partner—but he must be prepared to learn.'

Perhaps if we could find an 'apostolic Christian' he would argue in this way. It would certainly not be easy to defend a departure from the New Testament's varieties of ministry to our present rigid pattern. Surely nothing but good can come from taking one step back towards the richness of a varied ministry.

Notes to Chapter 4

[1] Douglas Webster: Patterns of Part Time Ministry in some churches in South America (World Dominion Press, 1964) page 40.
[2] cf Denis Lawton: Social Class Language and Education (Routledge Kegan Paul, 1968) pages 77–102.
[3] A Supporting Ministry (Church Information Office, 1968).
[4] Patterns of Part Time Ministry, page 16.

5   Its Necessity

This book began with a simple limited objective: to describe an attempt which has been made to find a pattern of ministry suited to our needs in East London. In the event, it has been impossible to explain the plan without stating the wider issue, the alienation of the working class from the church.

A majority of the population of England is alienated from the Christian church. For many, this alienation is not the result of having rejected the claims of Christ. They are prevented from making that crucial choice by considerations which are social, not spiritual. Faced by a body which is almost entirely middle class in its attitudes, working class people automatically assume that for them it is irrelevant. The reasons for this instinctive reaction are deeply buried in the history of our society. The fact must be faced. It is a moral issue.

Bishop David Sheppard has isolated the issue in this way. A tiny minority of the urban English working class is associated with the church. Although these people constitute the largest social group in our population, they do not feel at home in the Body of Christ. Whose fault is it? The blame must rest in one of three places.

Is it God's fault? Perhaps He prefers one group of people to another. Does He care so little about so many that He designed the church in such a way as to include some and exclude others? Obviously not!

Well then, is it the fault of the people themselves? Are working class people unable to find a home in God's family because of some deficiency in themselves? Are they so sinful, stubborn or stupid that they have cut themselves off from the Body of Christ? Certainly not!

We are forced to the conclusion that it is our fault. It is the fault of the church if certain people do not feel that they belong there. For generations Christians of all denominations have made heroic sacrifices in East London. Yet no church can claim to be firmly rooted and secure. No progress will be made in solving this problem if we waste time trying to apportion blame, but those who constitute the family determine the nature and attitudes of the family. It can only be Christians themselves who are responsible, if social attitudes rather than spiritual issues favour some rather than others when the question is one of belonging to the church.

My limited objective, a book about a plan for local ministry, must in practice raise much wider issues about the nature of the church. Working class alienation demands a new kind of ministry. It also demands a new attitude in the church. Proposals for changes in the ministry provoke suggestions for changes in the church. Once the issue is accepted in these terms, it becomes something more than a problem of organization and administration. It is a moral and spiritual question. Is a working class church to be encouraged? The question is being forced on us in two ways.

1 The spirit of the age demands an answer

The spirit of our age can be defined in many ways. It is easy to be superficial; easier still, for Christians, to underline the bad and ignore the good. For the sake of our spiritual security, however, we need to define those attitudes in society which are in conflict with God. The Bible's strong and frequent warnings against worldliness are basically against the dangers of being pervaded by the spirit of the age. Christians are set in the midst of society yet called to be vitally different. The pictures are familiar: light, salt, leaven, all notable for their distinctive qualities. They influence their surroundings by imparting something significantly distinctive. Without that contribution the dark room, the flavourless food, the lifeless bread could not be what God intends.

God intends that His church should make a significantly distinctive contribution to society. To do so it must refuse to be pervaded by the spirit of the age. This means that while those around us prefer possessions we must emphasize the importance of giving. While the world prefers status, we embrace service. The spirit of the age covets esteem from men, we long for honour given by God. The Bible warns against worldliness so frequently and so strongly, simply because it is easier by far for Christians to share the world's attitudes than to stand against them. So easy, in fact, that it seems to be inevitable.

The lust for power is one aspect of the spirit of our age. Professor Tournier writes: 'The modern myth of power, of which Nietzsche is the chief prophet, is the philosophical expression of the process of power-concentration. The very formulation of the doctrine, however, accentuates the movement, persuading mankind as it does that power is the supreme value. For the respect for the human person, the protection of the weak, charity and the necessity of salvation by God, professed by Christianity, our age has substituted the cult of the State, the veneration of force, the crushing of the weak in the struggle for life, and confidence in the greatness of man, "ceaselessly climbing the ladder of progress and power".'[1]

When the church assumes that its leaders must come from the ranks of the decision makers who are used to being in positions of power, it is being pervaded by the spirit of the age, which is worldliness.

Again, the world is bound by the chain of affluence. We should be challenging this spirit. When we reflect it we are being worldly. Affluence breeds greed, just as it feeds on greed. Appetite can never be satisfied. Every new acquisition creates the desire for the next. The anticipated joy of possession turns to a frenzy of pursuing the unattainable. This attitude is nowhere more obvious than among those working class people who are just beginning to taste the pleasures of affluence.

The church has the tool to break this chain. Jesus said, 'It is more blessed to give than to receive'. In a world where no one does anything for nothing, voluntary clergy speak powerfully without saying a word. In His charge to the twelve before they left Him to preach and heal, Jesus said, 'You received without pay, give without pay' (Matthew 10.8).

The world worships status. The teaching profession and the youth service fight for status measured by academic yardsticks. When the church's ministers do the same, they are being pervaded by the spirit of the age. Society sees its leaders coming from certain social and educational 'layers' and not from others. The church should stand against this attitude, not reflect it.

Society worships achievement. The university place is the goal of the knowledge industry, once called education. Students are 'the cream of society'. The church reflects this attitude when it gives a disproportionate amount of its time and energy to evangelism among students. No one would presume to say that a graduate's soul was worth more than that of a coloured immigrant, of course. Nevertheless, an uncommitted observer may well deduce that this is the view of the church, on the evidence of the relative concern for students against the lack of work among immigrant groups.

We are being worldly when we assume that a wealthy church is a successful church; when we assume that it is promotion for a clergyman to move from the inner city to a wealthy suburb; whenever we say or think that 'middle class is better'. These are the attitudes of the world; our task is not to share but to stand against them. Worldliness is never far from the heart of the church. Not the paper tigers of the theatre and the pub but the real beast, which is often at our throat disguised in the shape of some of our most cherished assumptions.

If the church is even to begin to be seriously dedicated to fight for justice in the community, we must challenge the spirit of the age. The spirit of the age is worked out in the structures of society, and often reflected in the attitudes of the church. That is why working class alienation demands a new attitude in the church. The spirit of the age demands an answer. Are we ready for such a change?

2 God's word demands an answer

God's word has always been in conflict with tradition. Christ's ministry was a constant battle with a 'church' bound by tradition. He once told His opponents, 'For the sake of your tradition, you have made void the word of God' (Matthew 15.6).

Since then there has never been a time when Christians have not had to make a choice between tradition and God's word. If Paul had not won his struggle against the tradition of the Judaizers, there would be no Christian church today.

The tradition of our church is to ordain only one kind of clergyman. If we insist on that tradition, we make the word of God void, because Scripture knows nothing of such a settled tradition. The Bible encourages varieties of ministries, some paid some voluntary, some itinerant some local.

The tradition of our church is middle class. It assumes that a Christian will have ambitions to 'improve' himself. It teaches that middle class manners are a scriptural injunction rather than a cultural assumption. It encourages men to be respectable when Christ asks them to be obedient to Him.

When we prefer this tradition, we make void the word of God, because the Bible says that 'there is neither Jew nor Greek, there is neither slave nor free . . . you are all one in Christ Jesus' (Galatians 3.28).

God's word and the spirit of the age demand an answer to the question: does the alienation of the working class demand a change? If the answer is yes, it is yes not only to a new kind of ministry, but also to a new kind of church.

Note to Chapter 5
[1] Tournier, The Strong and the Weak (Student Christian Movement, 1963) page 160.

6 The Men's Eye View

arranged and edited by David Hewitt

The following pages are like a family photograph album. They contain snap shots of the different individuals' thoughts and reactions expressed at different stages during training. They are presented not only to add flesh and personality to the men, but also to indicate the distinctive contribution which they are and will be making to the ministry of the two churches. The material has been drawn from their log books and from a tape-recorded interview.

Beginnings and Call

'The thinking behind the scheme has come out of our own personal experience', in the context of growing frustration with the clergy-dominated structures of the Church. So the idea received the mental assent of each man straight away, and each one was keen to participate in the scheme, in spite of the initial uncertainty of its fulfilment; and in spite of 'the feeling of something in a glass case labelled "Be Careful: Under Experiment".'

Their calling to ordination came not as a 'blinding flash' but through being invited to take part in the training, through persevering with it, through a series of steps of personal commitment as the scheme began to flower, and through the seal placed on their call by both local and catholic Church. One man was fascinated by the glamour and status of the priesthood, but 'God in His own time confirmed my call for the right reasons. My object in serving Christ is to aim as high as my physical and mental capacities permit'. 'If it is His will, then I expect His backing'.

The significance of their call is that it has come *from* the local Church
and it will give them authority to minister *to* the local Church. This
was emphasized at the ballot in the two churches, an event which the
men anticipated with trembling. The results were correspondingly
uplifting. At the same time they realized that trust was being placed in
them by the people whom they hoped to serve, and this trust demanded
their respect. 'I am now assured of local support and can act with some
authority'. 'It was a boost to our morale; it makes me feel a greater
sense of responsibility'.

Looking ahead to ordination

'It will give us the confidence that we are accepted by the Church
universal!' 'Any authority I might have must be an authority of holiness,
of character, of competence'. 'The overwhelming ceremonial of the
ordination service would worry me, but I would accept it if
necessary'.

In East London it is considered a crime to make out that you are
socially or educationally 'a cut above' your relations and friends.
'I am totally opposed to any kind of dress that will mark me out as
different from the people to whom I will minister'. 'I'll still be the
same person, being used for a different purpose'.

'We must be aware of the danger of becoming one of Them, the
Vicar's yes-men, the danger of people putting us into a Vicar bracket'.
'My friend is a thermometer for me: he is for Supplementary Ministry
so long as we don't change character. He would soon let me know
if I got out of hand'.

The Point of the Scheme:
the Church and Working-Class People

'It is not a criticism of the existing clergy, but it *is* a criticism of the
Church's failure to use its manpower'. 'The imported minister is at a
disadvantage in East London because his knowledge of local culture
is second-hand'.

Class is a sensitive subject in whatever company it is discussed.

'The working man is something to be sneered at by the administrators. Two characteristics of the man who lives and works in this kind of so-called working-class area: first, his use of money; second, he would much rather collaborate with his fellows than compete with them'. But not everyone who lives in East London considers himself to be working-class. 'I wouldn't say that I am working-class, but I still represent and reflect the East End'.

'There is a similarity of pattern between the Church and Industry. As the bosses don't really know the minds of the workers, so the Church leaders don't know the minds of the people'. 'In the East End the Vicar and his family are in a world apart. Witness how long it has taken me to call the Vicar "Ted".'

'Where, oh where is that natural meeting-ground?' Yes, in East London as elsewhere the Church complains that people do not come to her services and meetings, while at the same time her members are failing to go out and meet people where they are, on neutral or even alien territory. 'How simple it is for the churches to become impervious to the world around, for Christians to miss the blindingly obvious because of our religious blinkers'.

'The Church is maimed by being a part of the Establishment, with no relevance to people's daily lives. People are happy to go along just using it when they need bolstering up'. 'Having found Christ in a direct and simple way I find it difficult to express my faith within the framework of the Church of England'. 'What do our services do? Whom do we cater for?' 'Our church is so unused to plain speaking; we cover up real feeling'.

'There is an idea that the working-class lacks leadership, that it has to be herded together and led by a ring in the nose. This scheme shows that ordinary blokes from the East End can take positions of authority. We must stand on our own feet and be truly indigenous'. 'Leadership in working-class areas can't be grafted on, it must spring from within'.

'A picture of working-class ministry: X preparing the Communion Table; starched linen cloth and shining silver; hands gnarled, broken nails, damaged skin. A focus of Christ'.

Part time, Unpaid Ministry

'We shall be full time ministers because we won't switch off when we go to work'. 'By continuing in our jobs we shall be more earthed to the world. This will be a better balance, more realistic'. 'Our ministry will be more natural because we already live here; other clergy come to live here only in order to minister'.

'If the Church doesn't pay me, this gives me more freedom to be an individual, though I will still submit to discipline'.

The question of time off and holidays is being thought about. The men are not expecting to exercise their ministry every evening of the week and every Sunday. 'We should have similar breaks from our church as the full time staff in order that we don't go stale'. After a tiring day's work it takes real determination and sacrifice to go out to a meeting, especially one which calls for preparation and leadership.

The Work of Ministry

'A priest, I have learned, is someone far removed from the TV image. He needs to be physically tough yet compassionate. The people whom Christ had a go at He also died for.' 'The job of smoothing ruffled feathers, being a peacemaker.' 'If we are to minister to others, then Christ must control us.'

I realized that people were depending on me for spiritual food—quite a frightening experience'. 'This sort of encounter (a hard frank talk with a friend) is what ministry is; a shattering effect. Heartbreak will be as much a part of the Christian minister's lot as will joy'. 'Building up a relationship is a lot harder and more painful than the "hit and run" type of Christian witness and evangelism'. 'Our neighbours know us as Christians and are watching us all the time'. 'How can I put myself into other people's shoes, sit where they sit, understand what they are saying?'

'It needs to be recognized that one man hasn't got all the gifts of the Spirit.' 'I can't see myself preaching, more pastoral care.' 'My gift is to be an administrator and to do youth work. I can't see myself helping people with deep personal problems, though this may develop in the future'. 'My gifts are in pastoral care; this is my life and pleasure. I do it easily and it fulfils me'. 'My task is to exercise an enabling ministry. This is already happening. Y (who used to be very reserved) can now run a Bible Study and lead Women's Fellowship'. 'I realize that as a team we complement each other'.

'When homes are used to win people for Christ, some things have to take second place—like washing up, cleaning, even meals at times. We prayed that our home would be used by the Lord. The strangest part is that it is mostly teenagers who are coming. All they seem to want is a cup of tea, to listen to records and to talk, sometimes until the early hours of the morning. Six people have come to Christ in our home'.

'I called on A and B. I do not intend to pressurize them into coming every Sunday. Even if they don't come to Church, I still wish to be a friend of the family. I fully believe that this couple will eventually come to Christ.'

'Far too much time is spent on discussions that could be more advantageously spent on evangelism'. 'I want to help people in our Church to plan more seriously for the future'.

The two men who have left the scheme aim to continue working and leading in their churches, much as they have been doing. The eventual aim of Supplementary Ministry is to build churches in which each member can minister in some way to the rest.

Pastoral Insights

'The problem of visiting when both parents go out to work and do overtime'. 'Lack of communication between neighbours in tower blocks'. 'The dangers of tongue-wagging'.

On chairing a PCC meeting: 'rather a frightening experience from behind the table'. 'I am learning to delegate and make others take responsibility'. 'The Lord gave me authority to answer'.

Most of the early opportunities for exercising leadership have come through group Bible Studies. 'There need to be more occasions for catering for mature Christians and not continually feeding babies'. 'My group leading was too autocratic; I encouraged people to depend on me'. 'Someone said to me that I did a good job in leading because I got others to speak and did not dominate the group. An answer to prayer!'

'If college lecturers use blackboards, overhead projectors, filmstrips etc., without people's intelligence being insulted, then I'm sure that visual aids can be used to good effect in Christian work'. 'Don't try to reconcile opposing ideas when they are obviously irreconcilable'. 'It's easier to talk about problems than to deal with them'.

'One must have understanding and sympathy towards such people as homosexuals, who are often not indulging wilfully'. 'We must love the unlovely and go where they are. It's easy to reject them. The difficult youngsters are the ones who need love'.

Speaking and Preaching

Speaking in public does not come easily. But its very pressure often lends an urgency and relevance less likely to come from the more highly polished performance of a regular minister. 'I sat on the edge of my seat waiting. My legs were shaking'. 'Petrified'. 'Nerve-racking and tough; wanting to be completely honest without exaggeration'. 'The most frightening experience of my life, to speak in the Church I had known all my life'. 'A number of people were generous with their praise. I was left with the feeling that I am a high-sounding windbag'. 'Z s talk was effective because it was *his story*, not just his theories'.

'My delivery needs improving'. 'I tried to cover too much ground'. 'Temptation to be glib and to create an image'. 'Important to be as natural as possible'. 'That baptism interview was like talking to a brick wall'.

The Bishop

The wise oversight and personal commitment of the Bishop of Stepney has been of crucial significance both to the scheme and to the men themselves. 'When he, our Bishop, spoke of confessing his misdeeds, it brought the man and the bishop so close to us'. 'He is in sympathy with us, involved with us. The difference in churchmanship did not seem to matter'. 'He said he felt drained spiritually, but the evening was full of fun'. 'He left us with much food for thought, as usual'.

'Some people speak from the mind to the mind. Others speak from the heart to the heart. The Bishop speaks from the will to the will— a will subjected to Christ's—so everything he says hits hard'.

The Training

They feel strongly that for them this 'apprenticeship' scheme has advantages both over full time college training and even over the type of course which is based on evening classes and weekends away.

(1) It does not seriously interfere with either their family life or their jobs.

(2) Instead of being concentrated, the training is spread out over a longer period, and consequently emphasizes that training itself is a continuing, lifelong process. 'Our whole life is a learning situation'.

(3) The training is geared specially for them and is adjustable. 'Instead of going through the mill (or 'sausage machine') we can, together with Ted, work out our own needs and capabilities'. 'We can pick the brains of the experts who come to us'.

(4) It is as much practical as academic. 'In this way we learn more about people and about our tools'.
 In fact, 'theologically we are as sound as most theological students, because we have had first-hand experience'.

On the other hand, 'it is difficult to find the time at home for three hours uninterrupted study; there's nowhere where you can cut your-self off completely. Once I had an evening set apart for study; then bang-bang at the door and there's X, and I am trying to make friends with him. After talking I sat up all night and tried to plough through the book with my eyes dropping'. One man can study in his lunch hours; others did not find this possible. 'I can't study in silence, it distracts me. We've been brought up in noise'. 'You've got to per-severe, even with interruptions; that is training in itself'.

The Academic Side of the Training

To say that the men are not academic is not at all the same thing as saying that they are not intelligent. They may jib at unrelieved acres of print, but they are able to express well-informed, perceptive views on a wide range of subjects. 'If a lot of academic training had been required I'd have been counted out in the first round'. 'If we were too educated academically we'd get separated from the people we're serving'. 'No amount of stuffing the contents of dry books will make a Christian a better person spiritually'.

'I have little taste for disciplined study, which I acknowledge to be essential to the scheme. I absolutely dread the sessions'. One man did not find the material too difficult, another was baffled by 'the length of the words and their meaning'. 'Should it be decided that extra study and exams are essential to us, I should have to leave the scheme. Perhaps I should be devoting more time to people'.

'I thought I had a tolerable grasp of Scripture, but Canon Webster showed me I was still at kindergarten'. 'How to build a systematic working knowledge of the Bible?' 'The Bible is the only foundation we can build on and teach from'.

'Church History doesn't appeal to me.' Another found it 'a useful starter for further study, though not strictly necessary'. Another was fascinated to realize afresh that Jesus was a Jew, and all that this entailed.

The Group

Group consciousness is a vital part of the training; for it is one and the same group which is not only training together and putting that training into practice together now, but will also be continuing to minister together in the future.

At the first seminar 'I began learning from my fellow students: from A humility, from B analytical prowess, from C persistence, from D social conscience'. 'We are finding out each other's limitations, so we will be able to make allowances for each other in the future'.

The 'strength' of the group is constantly stressed, especially when one member is facing a daunting situation, such as preaching. 'The group training has given us authority and confidence'.

Loyalty to the group is therefore essential. 'My attitude as an individual has now been overtaken by my desire to preserve the group'. One man had to fulfil an alternative but important engagement, thus missing a group session which had been arranged for his benefit at a time which suited him. It was in fact possible for him to have met both engagements. He felt afterwards that he had offended and let down the others badly, and so he apologized publicly at the next meeting.

Shift work sometimes makes it hard to find a mutually convenient time to meet. Those who have to get up early for work carry a weight of tiredness. Tiredness leads easily to tensions. Frequently one member of the group feels left out. 'I feel the pressure of having to conform to a group discipline'. 'X did not express his support for me until afterwards. This was much too late and I told him so'. 'I used to resent Y and Z because of their greater knowledge. This came out in the form of aggression on my part'. 'A and I are close enough to insult each other frequently but not vehemently'.

The loss of two members of the group affected the others. 'When I first heard of it, for a moment I was pleased because I thought I would be more important and be given a greater say in things. I now feel very sad'. 'A personal loss; I could identify with him'.

'Honesty and plain speaking are the most important features of our group, taking our disagreements to each other'. 'You can perhaps hide in a pulpit, but not in this sort of group'. 'I have noticed recently how I can be dissected by the others and feel only a tiny bit aggrieved'.

'Being in a group brings out the individual. I can now appreciate B ten times more than I did a year ago. He probably hasn't changed much, but my relationship to him has changed'.

The Wives

'Unless she was 100% behind me from the beginning, I couldn't have started it. Both of us had to be committed'. 'Yes, you do get tensions'. 'It is very important that the wives join us for the three monthly Communion service and evening with the Bishop'. They also join their husbands for the occasional weekend away. In fact it is only their domestic duties which prevent them from attending more of the training.

Doubts and Conflicts

Each of the men has been assailed at various times by doubts concerning his own fitness and ability to continue with a scheme from which it is comparatively easy to withdraw at almost any stage.

One questioned his motives for joining the scheme. 'Are we going along for the ride, wishing to bask in the scheme's success (if it is successful)? Can I honour the commitment involved in view of my job and my home?' Another, recognizing his 'commitment problem' and 'unreliability', confessed, 'is this the stuff that ministers are made of?' 'I feel utterly worthless about my place in Supplementary Ministry. I don't even have the desire to complete my training, so with this attitude how can I become one of His priests?' 'I haven't made much of my life. I don't think I have ever converted anyone. I feel thoroughly useless and empty, and a hypocrite as well'.

'Now that the ACCM Selection Conference is drawing nearer I am getting an awful emptiness in my stomach at the prospect. If I am unsuitable it will be a great disappointment'. 'While my mind accepted the possibility of rejection, my emotions certainly didn't.'

Here is one strong and persistent distraction. 'One gets the temptation to move away from our part of London, for the sake of one's family, into a more pleasant-looking community. I have been thinking very much about the education of my children. Would they do better away from East London?' 'We consider ourselves settled here, but seeing our friends' new house and semi-rural setting the old devil started his tricks. We thought how nice it would be to get away from the noise and smoke. But we were reminded that the Lord wants us here, and here we stay until He says otherwise'.

Beside their home, their job is another vital part of their lives. Relationships at work test a man, and so does any degree of insecurity in his job. 'My increasing isolation in a large group of people that I work with. I can do nothing but continue to live my life according to my Christian principles, accepting that God must know what He is doing'. 'Is it really right for me to remain in a manual job as a Supplementary Minister? My almost constant back trouble makes it painful for me to lift anything. To leave my present job would mean a drop in income. Whatever job I do I would want to be involved with people. To be even an assistant social worker one needs to have various degrees or diplomas. To know what to do is a problem, but with Christ's help I know this will be overcome'.

One man felt condemned because he had been working with someone for nearly three weeks before the man realized that he was a Christian, and then only when he was observed reading a religious book.

Knowledge of God, Self and Others

'There is nowhere I can go and be away from Christ'. 'I am conscious of the Lord at all times, life without Him is nothing'. 'I must learn to be so Christ-centred that I behave naturally'. 'In devotional life evangelicals have an easy upbringing; so I am most undisciplined. You don't get out any more than you put in. But should I conform to a pattern that is not natural to me?'

'No part of my life is lived to the full'. 'I must learn not to be afraid of failure'. 'I am aware how unkind and unfeeling I can be'. 'My cynicism, instant summing up of people; a semi-detached person'. 'Impatience at being bogged down with technical clutter'. 'I must learn that there is a time to say "I don't know" about such questions as the mystery of suffering'. 'Knowledge is to be used and applied, not displayed'.

'Since my own acceptance of myself I now feel more accepted by others'. 'Witnessing to my family has been very difficult. Tempers are never far away. I find it easier with strangers. Yet I have a great love for my family'.

'Others are not necessarily wrong because they are different from me—complementary not contradictory'. 'Those whom I have labelled black have good points I must look for'. 'I must remember his background and make allowances'. 'To be let down without notice is to be taken for granted, it expresses a familiarity which is beyond the normal bounds of fellowship'. 'He did not want to hear my story and I began to lose confidence in him. We should listen to all that people have to say, show interest and then help them if at all possible'. 'In my reading of the New Testament I keep being jabbed in the face by "love all men".'

Conclusion

Many of the remarks made in this chapter unearth a deep sense of inadequacy, which stems from the feeling that they fail to measure up to the educational standard and general image demanded of a clergyman in the Church of England. How many other people are barred from exercising their gifts in the Church by this same sense of inadequacy?

And yet, simply through living out his life in the rough and tumble of a working-class area, many a person acquires gifts of ministry and leadership which can never be picked up on an academic course. So there are rich resources in and around our Church life which are waiting to be tapped. It is hoped that these men will, among other things, act as a bridge between clergy and working-class people, and that this bridge will carry much traffic—in both directions.

Postscript

It is impossible to produce even a slim volume like this without involving a large number of one's friends in the process. It is because most of these helpers are friends and not paid assistants, that the need arises to acknowledge them; it is the least one can do.

The first debt I acknowledge, however, is not to a friend but to someone I have never met Roland Allen. I wish he were still alive to see the effect his prophetic books are now having, as he predicted fifty years ago. David Sheppard has provoked and enlightened me consistently for ten years. Any worthwhile thinking behind these words has been fed to me by him, though he cannot be held responsible when it has been badly digested.

There are a number of people without whom there would be no scheme about which to write. Bishop Trevor has consistently backed us from the moment the idea first landed in his lap two months after his arrival from Africa. It is a measure of the man that in the midst of all the pressure of readjustment he was prepared to promise support unhesitatingly, and has continued to give it from that day to this.

These two Bishops, Woolwich and Stepney, called together a dozen people from their respective areas to discuss working class ministry, and I have learned a great deal from that group in two years. I have drawn heavily on a document which they produced, in fact most of it is quoted here in one form or another.[1]

It goes without saying that there are six people who have been essential to this story, the men who have belonged to the team: Bill Harrap, Richard Hayward, Gordon Kendall, Jack Page, David Rudiger and Henry Watson. My full-time colleagues, Margaret Fish, Alan Seabrook and David Hewitt have shown great faith and unselfishness in the way they have welcomed Supplementary Ministry.

The congregations of the two churches have been amazingly ready to work through the consequences as we have taken each step together.

All those already named (except Roland Allen!) helped by reading the draft. In addition, Jackie Burgoyne, Roger Dowley, Jean Hewitt, Harry Hill, John Tanburn, Peter Yacomeni, John Hunter and Timothy Dudley-Smith took great trouble offering creative criticism. Hugh Fearn, Warden and Chairman of the Readers' Board for London, gave valuable support and encouragement to the scheme in its early days.

The Brethren and Sisters of the Royal Foundation of St Katharine, Stepney, cossetted me so that I was able to do the writing to a tight schedule, and my wife tolerated me when, in the toils of authorship, I was more than usually intolerable.

---

[1] Local ministry in urban and industrial areas (Mowbrays, 1972).

LOUD
and clear

A practical handbook on local church publicity
Simon Webley & John Capon

Utterly practical and realistic, this book by an
Anglican and a Baptist spells out the need for local
churches to take publicity in all its forms seriously.
It is full of facts, suggestions and information. It
explains why and tells how. No outward looking
group of Christians can fail to find this book useful
and some may find it revolutionary.

One People

Voted *CRUSADE* magazine's 'book of the month' when first published John Stott's examination of teamwork in the ministry of the local church has been widely read and praised.

As with other books in this series, the author blends his theology and theory with solid examples of what has been put into practice. He strongly criticises clericalism but believes there is a distinctive role for the ordained ministry in the modern Church.

'We are building synodical "castles in the air". This book could help us to put foundations under them.'
The Bishop of Liverpool in CEN

'It might . . . lead to a revival of true religion within a generation.'
Church Times

MINISTRY
IN THE SEVENTIES

How can the Church cope with the next few years? Some
say it must die and be reborn. Some say that the house
must replace the archaic edifice. In this book a team
of Evangelical thinkers representing all sections of
Church life face up to such issues as urbanization,
multiracialism, shrinking but continuing rural life,
the communication question and other matters. Their
essays are rooted to realities and packed with practical
suggestions.

Reaching the Families

Michael Botting

The Bishop of London in his foreword writes:
'This is a book of real importance because it is
writtten against the background of deep pastoral
care and prayerful experiment. Its author has
faced the problems of communicating the Faith
and winning souls for Christ in an area where
churchgoing is the exception and not the rule,
and where only a small percentage of the people
has any real commitment to the Christian faith.'

Open House

This is far more than the account of an experiment in home meetings. John Tanburn feels deeply that there needs to be a revolution in local church structures and ruthlessly analyses what he considers to be the shortcomings of accepted patterns.

This is a provocative book and many may disagree with it, but nobody could fail to be the better off for having faced up to its challenges and suggestions.

'Forty-five new penceworth of sanctified, practical commonsense'—*Church Times*

'. . . the book is bound to stimulate'—*Church of England Newspaper*

'. . . . a thrilling story and the cogent argument for the house church in our day is something which . . . every local church should read and consider'—*Floodtide*

Foreword by the Bishop of Rochester